Acknowledgments

Author	John Dawkins
Editorial Director	Donald R. Senter, Ed.D.
Editors-in-Chief of Basic Skills	Irwin F. Harris Helen Frackenpohl Morris
Project Editors	Estelle Kleinman Elizabeth Zayatz
Editorial Assistant	Agatha Mingolello
Art Director	Ronald J. Wickham
Editing Supervisor	Steven J. Griffel
Designer	Patricia Kovic
Art Production Coordinator	Carol Kaplan
Production Assistant	Michele Rios-Guzman

ISBN 1-55855-678-8

10 11 12 13 DBH 04 03 02 01

Contents

Extension Activities

This new edition of the Write and Read Study Guide contains an Extention Activity for each lesson that reinforces the writing and reading skills taught in the lesson. The writing activities are based on the reading comprehension skills taught in Reading Strategies and the Language Clues vocabulary. These Extension Activities can be used either as a follow-up activity or for review and reinforcement after some time has lapsed. Extension activities begin on page 123.

To the Student

Introduction

Welcome to the EDL Write and Read program. The lessons in this book will help you improve your writing and reading skills by learning:

- How to write a complete sentence
- How to punctuate sentences correctly
- How to be sure that subjects and verbs go together
- How to write a good paragraph

Each lesson is organized in a step-by-step manner. First you are given instruction in a skill with plenty of examples. Next you are given practice in the skill. When you have mastered the skill, you go on to a new skill. You then receive instruction and practice in *that* skill. You are given a chance to check your mastery of each skill before moving on to the next one. This book also gives you a chance to use your newly learned skills in writing and reading activities.

General Directions for Completing Lessons

Read carefully when you work in this book. Think about what you read. Study the examples. If you don't understand something, ask your teacher to explain.

Read all directions carefully.

Write all your answers on your answer sheet.

Check your answers with the Answer Key. If you get an answer wrong, look back to see why you are wrong. If you can't figure out why you're wrong, ask your teacher. It's possible that there is more than one right answer.

Agreement Problems

When Is Agreement a Problem?

When verbs are in the past tense there is usually no agreement problem. The verb stays the same with either a singular or plural subject:

One sandwich **tasted** good to Thomas.
Two sandwiches **tasted** good to Vivian.

The verb *be* is an exception. It has two forms for past:

One sandwich **was** all he wanted.
Two sandwiches **were** all she wanted.

All other agreement problems happen only with the present tense:

One sandwich **tastes** good.
Two sandwiches **taste** good.

Compound Subjects

Compound subjects are usually plural, so they take the plural form of the verb:

Compound subjects	Plural verbs

The employer and employee **work** together.
The book and pencil **are** on the table.

Sometimes compound subjects are not considered plural. This happens when the two subjects are really acting as a team. They have a singular meaning. Look at this example:

Singular verb

Bacon and eggs **makes** a good breakfast.

It is not the bacon alone or the eggs alone that makes a good breakfast. It is the **team** of bacon and eggs that makes a good breakfast.

Now look at this example:

Bacon and eggs were on sale today.

In this case, the bacon and eggs are not acting as a team. Instead, they form a compound subject and therefore take the plural form of the verb. You can tell that *bacon and eggs* form a compound subject because you can break this sentence into two sentences without losing the original meaning of the sentence:

Bacon was on sale today.
Eggs were on sale today.

....

See if you can do the next two. Rewrite each sentence using the correct verb form.

1. Toast and jelly (is, are) not much of a lunch. _____

_____

2. Toast and jelly (is, are) two foods I don't like. _____

_____

Did you find that the subjects in example 1 act as a team? In that case the compound subject takes the singular form of the verb. In example 2, the two subjects do not act as a team. They take the plural form of the verb.

Practice

Rewrite each sentence using the correct verb form.

3. Cake and donuts (is, are) good for desert. _____

_____

4. A cat and dog (sleeps, sleep) in the sun on the porch. _____

_____

5. Peaches and cream (tastes, taste) good anytime. _____

_____

6. A horse and buggy (is, are) coming down the street. _____

_____

Or and Nor

When a compound subject is joined by *or*, the verb is singular:

A dog **or** cat **makes** a good pet.

It's easy to see why you use the singular verb. The meaning is "one of them, not both."

The conjunction *nor* is a little different, but it also takes a singular verb. Nor is a type of negative, and it means "none of those mentioned":

Neither Jill **nor** Ellen **is** going.

The meaning of the sentence seems to point to the compound subject because it is almost like saying *Jill and Ellen are not going.* Even so, *nor* takes a singular verb.

This is strange.

Rule 1

When a compound subject is joined by *or* or *nor*, the verb is singular.

Practice

Rewrite each sentence using the correct verb form.

7. Dobrinsky or Carline (is, are) going on that dangerous mission. _____

_____

8. The employer or the foreman (inspects, inspect) the new building each morning. _____

_____

9. Only Jack or Mario (has, have) a chance of getting that job.

_____

10. Neither candy nor ice cream (has, have) ever helped anyone lose weight. _____

_____

More about Or *and* Nor

Sometimes you might get confused when one of the subjects in a compound subject is singular and the other is plural:

Two cats or one dog (is, are) all I can have at one time.
Neither Pam nor her sisters (sings, sing) in the chorus.

In cases like these, the verb agrees with the subject nearer the verb:

Two cats or **one dog is** all I can have at one time.
Neither Pam nor **her sisters sing** in the chorus.

....

The same is true for pronouns:

Either she or **they are** picking you up.
Neither he nor **I go** home before 4:00.

**Rule 2**

When a singular and a plural subject are joined by *or* or *nor*, the verb agrees with the subject nearer the verb.

Practice

Rewrite each sentence using the correct verb form.

11. Neither the cat nor the dogs (knows, know) when to say no to food. _____
_____

12. Either he or we (is, are) to get the prize. _____
_____

13. Either the boys or Betty (is, are) knocking on the door. ____
_____

When Subjects Come After Verbs

Sometimes the subject of a sentence comes after the verb. When this happens, the first thing you have to do is find the subject. What is the subject of the following sentence?

What's the subject? ○ ○ ○ There (is, are) two questions that I can't answer.

The subject is *two questions*. Since *two questions* is plural, you must use the plural form of the verb:

Subject

There **are** two questions that I can't answer.

Here are some more examples:

Subject

Here *are* the **two Cokes** you wanted.

Subject

Where *is* **the hamburger**?

Practice

Rewrite each sentence using the correct verb form.

14. Where (is, are) the architect who is responsible for the poor structure of this building? _____

_____

15. There (is, are) many historical buildings in Trenton. _____

_____

16. Where (is, are) the dome on the Capitol? _____

_____

17. Near the river (is, are) the state buildings. _____

_____

Confusing Phrases

Look at this sentence:

One of the boys is sleeping.

The complete subject is *one of the boys*. But what is the main word in the subject? It's *one*. *Of the boys* is a phrase that modifies *one*. The verb must agree with the main word in the subject. Don't let the phrases that come be-

tween confuse you:

One of the boys **is** sleeping.

Don't be fooled by long phrases. Always look for the main word of the subject, and make sure that the verb agrees with it.

The **man** with the black jacket and blue pants **is** looking at you.

Practice

Rewrite each sentence using the correct verb form.

18. One of the writers (has, have) written about the local farmers. _____

_____

19. The woman with the small baby in her arms (is, are) my wife. _____

_____

20. People in that country (chooses, choose) their leaders by voting. _____

_____

Rewriting Sentences

You will come up with agreement problems as you write. At times, you may want to rework your sentence to get rid of the problem.

For example, notice how these sentences have been changed so that the problem disappears:

One big Coke or two small Cokes (is, are) a lot to drink.
One big Coke or two small Cokes will be a lot to drink.

Neither he nor you (is, are) to leave the room till after lunch.
Neither he nor you can leave the room till after lunch.

....

Notice that we changed the verb by using a helping verb that had no agreement problem.

Another way to rewrite the sentence is to get rid of the *nor*, like this:

You and he are not to leave the room until after lunch.

By changing the *nor* compound to an *and* compound, we have made the agreement problem simple.

There are many ways to rewrite sentences. Don't give up too quickly. For example, here's another way:

One thing you two are not going to do is leave the room until after lunch.

Practice

Rewrite each sentence so that there is no longer a problem of agreement between the subject and verb.

21. A dog or a cat always (makes, make) a good gift for a child.

_____

22. Either the architect or the construction workers (is, are) at the building site. _____

_____

23. Neither you nor I (am, are) ready for the inspection. _____

_____

24. You or Joey (was, were) going to teach Elsi how to throw a Frisbee. _____

_____

More Practice

Rewrite each sentence using the correct verb form.

1. Ice cream and Coke (is, are) not a good lunch! _____

_____

2. There (has, have) been many problems in the world this year.

_____

continued

3. I knew one of the local farmers (was, were) growing corn for hogs. _____

4. The doctors talking with the tall nurse (wants, want) help in room 804. _____

5. Neither I nor my sisters (is, are) going to be home for Thanksgiving. _____

6. Either my mother or some great Mexican cook (has, have) made these tamales. _____

7. The hamburger and two pizzas (is, are) ready to go. _____

8. After each game there (is, are) some fans asking for autographs. _____

9. Pizza and hamburgers (is, are) my favorite foods. _____

10. One of those men (plays, play) the guitar. _____

11. Only one art student out of ten (wants, want) to be an architect. _____

More Agreement Problems

Collective Nouns

Collective nouns are nouns that stand for a group, such as these:

army	class	crew	herd	pair
audience	club	crowd	jury	public
band	committee	family	mob	squad
choir	company	gang	nation	team
chorus	couple	group	orchestra	troop

Each of these nouns can mean the group as a whole—one single collection—in which case the meaning is singular and the singular form of the verb is used.

The family was seated at the table.

In this case the family as one unit was seated at the table. But now look at another example where *the family* is the subject of a sentence:

The family were taking their seats at the table.

In this case, the noun refers to the individual members of the group, so the meaning is plural.

Notice that the plural form of the verb has been used.

The difference between the singular meaning and plural meaning is not always easy to see. It is often just a matter of how the writer sees it. It helps if there is a pronoun or other word in the sentence that means singular or plural:

The family **were** taking **their** seats at the table.

The family **was** seated in **its** living room.

The pair **were brothers**.

Practice

Rewrite each sentence using the correct verb form. Look for pronouns or nouns in the sentence that will give you clues to whether the subject is singular or plural.

1. The team (is, are) posing for its picture. _____

_____

2. The typical crew on a pirate ship (was, were) criminals. ____

_____

3. The public (was, were) amazed by the film on falling meteors.

_____

4. The audience (shows, show) its amazement at the exhibit on

solar energy. _____

continued

5. The scout troop (is, are) pitching their tents. _____

_____

6. The jazz band (has, have) a definite style. _____

_____

7. The orchestra (waits, wait) quietly for its conductor to appear.

_____

Rewriting to Avoid Problems

Which verb form would you choose for the following sentence?

The orchestra (waits, wait) quietly for their conductor.

You would choose the plural verb form *wait* because the word *their* has a plural meaning. But *the orchestra wait* sounds odd to many people. So they avoid it and write this:

The members of the orchestra wait quietly for their conductor.

There is no confusion here because the main word of the subject is now *members*, which is clearly plural. This even seems to give a better picture of the individual musicians.

So one way to avoid collective noun problems when you write is to rewrite the sentence to avoid them. You can do this by: 1) adding a subject that is clearly plural, and 2) making the collective noun part of a prepositional phrase. Look at these examples:

The team have taken their showers.	**The members of** the team have taken their showers.
The gang like pizza.	**The boys in** the gang like pizza.

Think of a plural subject.

Practice

Rewrite each sentence to avoid the problems of plural agreement with a collective noun. Add a subject that is clearly plural and make the collective noun part of a prepositional phrase.

Then choose the plural verb forms.

8. The class (is, are) studying nitrogen, hydrogen, and carbon in their science books. _____

_____

9. The chorus (have, has) a genuine liking for their leader. ___

_____

10. The team (agree, agrees) that they should practice more. ___

_____

11. The club (vote, votes) on how to spend their money. _____

Nouns of Quantity

Nouns of quantity are plural nouns of measure, figures, money, etc. Here are some examples:

three months
five gallons
two hours
ten cents

As with collective nouns, whether a noun of quantity is singular or plural depends on how the writer views it. But there are some guidelines that will help you decide. They are much like those for collective nouns.

When a noun of quantity represents one single unit, singular verbs are used.

Twenty cents is what the candy costs.
Five gallons is all the gas I need.
A hundred yards is a long way to run.

Which verb form would you use in the following sentence?

Ten dollars (is, are) all I have to my name.

Ask yourself: Is ten dollars a single thing or is it ten different things? It is a single thing. We're talking about ten dollars as a whole. So you should use the singular form of the verb—is.

In general, these nouns of quantity are considered singular. But if you are thinking of the separate parts of the whole quantity, then your subject can be plural:

Two weeks of vacation **are** coming up.
Twenty pennies have fallen on the floor.
Seven acres were plowed last spring.

Practice

Rewrite each sentence using the correct verb form.

12. Five more dollars (gives, give) the woman ten dollars. ____
_____

13. A hundred pounds (is, are) not much for a fifteen-year-old boy. _____
_____

14. Sixty-five years (is, are) an average lifetime. _____
_____

15. Ten feet of fence (is, are) what I need. _____
_____

16. Seven quarters (is, are) going into my piggy bank. _____
_____

More about "of" Phrases

You have learned that the verb should agree with the main word of the subject. This means that it should not agree with a phrase or other noun that modifies the subject. For example,

look at these:

The **students** from Texas **are** waiting.

The **stores** on the street **were** open.

But there is a special group of words that depend on the prepositional phrase to make them singular or plural. And the prepositional phrase in this type of sentence always begins with *of*. Look at this sentence:

All of my friends (is, are) coming to my party.

The main word of the subject—*all*—doesn't mean singular or plural. To find out if it has a singular or plural meaning, you must look at the noun in the prepositional phrase.

All of my **friends are** coming to my party.

Since *friends* is plural, the plural form of the verb is used.

Here are some more examples where the verb agrees with the noun in the prepositional phrase:

All of the **story was** interesting.

All of the **stories were** interesting.

A lot of **children catch** colds on Halloween.

A lot of **milk is** wasted.

Three-fourths of the **world is** hungry.

Three-fourths of the **people are** hungry.

....

The following is a list of some of the words that depend on the prepositional phrase to make them singular or plural:

all	half
none	one-half, two-thirds
any	(and all fractions)
some	lot
more	part
most	

Practice

Rewrite each sentence using the correct verb form. If the main word of the subject is one of the special words you just learned about, choose the verb that agrees with the noun in the prepositional phrase. In all other cases, choose the verb that agrees with the main word of the subject.

17. Some of the meteors (burns, burn) up in space. _____

_____

18. All of the meteor (burn, burns) up in space. _____

_____

19. The streets of the city (is, are) dangerous. _____

_____

20. Half of the food (is, are) good. _____

_____

continued →

21. Two-thirds of the students (like, likes) rock music. _____

_____

22. The men in the story (was, were) aliens from another planet.

_____

Nouns That End in *-s* or *-ics*

You can have agreement problems with nouns that end in *-s* or *-ics*. The first group of these words is almost always singular even though the word looks plural.

Physics is my favorite.
Measles is going around my school.

Here is a list of most of the nouns that look plural, but take a singular verb:

gymnastics	linguistics
physics	mathematics
civics	measles
economics	news

Some nouns that end in *-s* take the plural verb even though they refer to one thing.

The **scissors were** lost.

Lucky for us, there are just a couple of these:

pants
trousers
scissors
tweezers

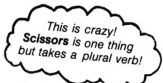
This is crazy! *Scissors* is one thing but takes a plural verb!

And a few other nouns that end in *-s* are usually singular but might sometimes be plural. You must look at the meaning of the sentence to know which verb form to use. For example, read the following sentences:

A. **Politics is** interesting every four years.
B. The two Presidents' **politics were** very different.

In sentence A, the writer is talking about politics as a single unit, so the singular form of the verb is used. In sentence B, the writer is talking about the politics of **two** Presidents. Since here *politics* means more than one, the plural verb form was used.

Here are some more examples. Can you figure out why each noun is considered singular or plural?

Athletics is for young people.
All **athletics are** offered at Poly High.
Statistics is studied in college.
His **statistics** last season **were** not very good.

Practice

Rewrite each sentence using the correct verb form.

23. Economics (is, are) her specialty. _____

_____

24. His pants (is, are) too long. _____

_____

25. The news (is, are) all bad. _____

_____

continued →

26. The tweezers (is, are) on the table. _____

_____

27. Her statistics (does, do) not agree with yours. _____

_____

More Practice

Rewrite each sentence using the correct verb form.

1. The class (is, are) having its lunch in the park. _____

_____

2. The family (plans, plan) to save their money for a vacation.

_____

3. Four inches (is, are) a lot to grow in one year. _____

_____

4. One-third of the cake (is, are) yours. _____

_____

5. Some of the fire fighters (wants, want) to go on strike. _____

_____

6. The scissors (is, are) in the sewing box. _____

_____

7. Measles (is, are) not a serious disease these days. _____

_____

8. Three weeks (has, have) gone by since I ordered that book.

_____

9. Most of my time (is, are) spent on important matters. _____

_____

10. The student committee (has, have) voted for their class president. _____

_____

Agreement with Indefinite Pronouns

Indefinite Pronouns

This is the last lesson on agreement. It is a lesson that can cause even careful writers trouble, a lesson about **indefinite pronouns**. These pronouns are called "indefinite" because the person or things they point to are usually general—not very definite. Here are some examples:

Scott looked at the audience. He didn't see **anyone** he knew.
Tina looked around the store. **Everything** looked OK.

There are three groups of indefinite pronouns:

1. These are considered plural:

    both   few   many   several

2. These are almost always considered singular:

everyone	anyone	someone	no one	each	one
everybody	anybody	somebody	nobody	either	another
everything	anything	something	nothing	neither	

3. The last group may be singular or plural, depending upon your meaning:

any	none	most	part	two-thirds
all	some	the rest	half	three-fourths

    You saw some of these in the last lesson.

We will look at these groups one at a time.

Always Plural

These indefinite pronouns clearly mean "more than one," so it is easy to see why they should agree with the plural form of the verb:

both   few   many   several

These all take plural verbs.

Here is how *few* is used:

Many criminals receive punishment for their crimes. **Few** are condemned to die.

What does *few* point back to? *Few* points back to *criminals*, and *criminals* is clearly a plural noun. So *few* takes the plural verb form *are condemned*.

Many **criminals** receive punishment for their crimes. **Few are**

condemned to die.

Here is how *several* is used:

Policewoman Thatcher has caught many criminals. **Several** were very dangerous.

1. What noun does *several* point back to? _____
   a. Policewoman   b. Thatcher   c. criminals

2. What verb does *several* agree with? _____
   a. has caught   b. was   c. were

Here is how *both* is used:

I have two good pens at home. **Both** work beautifully.

3. What does *both* point back to? _____
   a. I   b. two good pens   c. home

4. What verb does *both* agree with? _____
   a. have   b. is   c. work

And here is how *many* works:

Judge Gates has heard federal trials all her life, and **many** have required that a jury be selected.

5. What does *many* point back to? _____
   a. Judge Gates   b. federal trials   c. a jury

6. What verb does *many* agree with? _____
   a. have required   b. has heard   c. be selected

Sometimes you won't find the noun or noun phrase that the indefinite pronoun points back to. This makes no difference. You still always use the plural form of the verb.

José loves everything about his life. **Few are** as happy as he is.

In this case few could mean a number of things—men, people, children, etc. But everything that *few* could mean has a plural meaning. So it is still logical that the word *few* takes a plural verb.

Practice

Rewrite each sentence using the correct verb form.

Only rewrite the second sentence here.

7. Officer Crowell answers complaints every day, and many (deals, deal) with mistreated children. _____

_____

8. I have two younger brothers, and both (looks, look) like me.

_____

9. Martha can dance, run, write, climb, and play drums. Few (is, are) able to do all that she can. _____

_____

10. That group cut many records over the years, and several (was, were) very popular. _____

_____

Almost Always Singular

A lot of pronouns are almost always considered singular. But it isn't too hard to remember which ones they are. Many of them are made the same way. They start like this:

>   every-   any-   some-   no-

Then add -*one*, -*body*, or *thing*:

everyone	anyone	someone	no one
everybody	anybody	somebody	nobody
everything	anything	something	nothing

There are only a few of these pronouns that are not formed this way. They are:

>   each   one
>   either   another
>   neither

All of these pronouns usually take a singular verb.

Everyone respects the supreme court.
Anything tastes better than Doc's Supreme Orange Drink.

Write the verb you would use for the following sentences:

11. Of all the players I have ever played with, nobody (play, plays) harder than Harrison

Tweed. _____

12. Somebody (have, has) identified Jason as

the criminal. _____

Now let's look at some sentences where there is a second pronoun that must agree with the indefinite pronoun.

Everyone here likes **his or her** work.

> *His or her is singular.*

Since *Everyone* is singular, the pronoun that refers to it must also be singular.

Look at another example. Which pronoun would you use?

Nobody wants people to tease (him or her, them).

Since *Nobody* is singular, you should choose the singular pronoun—*him or her*. However, many people might think that using *them* sounds better. They're probably right about that, but using *them* is generally not considered correct for written English. There is a way out. You can rewrite the sentence to avoid using *him or her*.

Nobody wants people to tease him or her.
Nobody wants to be teased.
OR
People don't want to be teased by others.

Practice

Rewrite each sentence doing two things: 1) Use the correct verb form(s), and 2) use the correct pronoun form. If you choose, you can rewrite the sentence to avoid using awkward wording such as *he or she*.

13. Everyone (wants, want) (his or her, their) children to be

good students. _____

_____

_____

continued →

14. Two girls are on the baseball team, but neither (thinks, think) that (she, they) can be the team's best player. _____

_____

_____

15. Everything that (fits, fit) me looks as if (it, they) (is, are) out of style. _____

_____

_____

16. No one (likes, like) to get into an argument with (his or her, their) parents. _____

_____

_____

17. Nobody in the police department (has, have) the authority to punish the criminal (he or she, they) (arrests, arrest). ____

_____

_____

The Exceptions

Sometimes the meaning of a sentence changes so that it becomes silly to use a singular pronoun to agree with the indefinite pronoun. Look at an example:

Singular   Singular

Everyone in the class **has** sent Ms. Fitch a get-well card, and she has sent thank-you cards to (him or her, them).

The second pronoun does refer back to *Everyone*, but there is no sense in making that second pronoun singular. The meaning is that she sent thank-you cards to **all the members of the class.** Because of this, you should use the plural pronoun form—*them.*

Which pronoun form would you use in this example?

Mr. and Mrs. Cross ran out of the house screaming "Fire!" The children ran out crying. **Everyone was** crazy. Finally, I told (him or her, them) all to relax.

Because of the meaning of these sentences, the second pronoun is talking about Mr. and Mrs. Cross and their children. Using a singular pronoun would be silly, so you should use the plural pronoun—*them.*

Practice

Rewrite each sentence doing two things: 1) Use the correct verb form(s), and 2) use the correct pronoun form. If you choose, you can rewrite the sentence to avoid using awkward wording such as *he or she.*

18. Ezra has given his speech before twenty other students, and everyone (say, says) he was good. In fact, (he or she, they) (wants, want) him to speak again. _____

_____

_____

Here's a clue: Only one of these sentences takes a singular pronoun.

19. No one (was, were) surprised when Ms. Crane entered her plea of guilty; in fact, (he or she, they) would have been surprised if she didn't plead guilty. _____

_____

_____

20. No one likes to pay for a parking ticket that (he or she, they) didn't deserve. _____

_____

21. Everyone (was, were) helping Mr. Fritzky fix up his new house, and he appreciated (his or her, their) efforts. _____

_____

_____

Singular or Plural

Some indefinite pronouns can be singular or plural depending on what they refer to. Here is a list of some of these pronouns:

any	none	most	part	two-thirds
all	some	the rest	half	three-fourths

Look at this sentence:

I've eaten many **pies**, but I don't know **any** that **are** as good as these.

Since *any* refers back to the plural noun *pies*, it takes the plural verb *are.*

Now look at this sentence:

I know you spent a lot of **money** yesterday. Tell me if **any is** left.

In this case *any* refers to the singular noun *money*, so it takes the singular verb *is*.

Here are two more examples:

Singular

All the **food has** been eaten.

Plural

All the **cards have** fallen off the table.

Practice

Rewrite each sentence using the correct verb form.

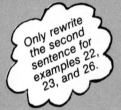

Only rewrite the second sentence for examples 22, 23, and 26.

22. I disliked the meat. Most of it (was, were) raw. _____

_____

23. We ate the apples. Most (was, were) good. _____

_____

24. Three-fourths of the cake (was, were) gone. _____

_____

25. Midge didn't think that any of the boys in school (was, were) her age. _____

_____

26. The king had great wealth. Part (was, were) in Switzerland; part (was, were) in New York. _____

_____

More Practice

Rewrite each sentence using the correct verb and/or pronoun forms. If you choose, you can rewrite the sentence to avoid using awkward wording.

1. Mr. Gordon liked everyone who (was, were) in his tenth-grade health class; he just wished (he or she, they) would keep quiet.

_____

_____

2. Everyone in the class (wasn't, weren't) fond of rock music; Franklin knew several who (was, were) Beethoven fans. _____

_____

_____

continued

3. Anyone who (knows, know) anything about law (knows, know) that anyone (is, are) innocent until proven guilty. ___

_____

_____

4. Maria ate one-eighth of the pie; the rest (was, were) left over.

_____

_____

5. Junk foods might taste good, but most (is, are) of no value.

_____

_____

6. Pete and Bill like the beach. Both (is, are) good swimmers.

_____

_____

Only write the second sentence for 6.

7. Everyone in this line (wants, want) (his or her, their) money back. _____

_____

8. Everything I write in English (turns, turn) out looking as if (it, they) (is, are) in Greek. _____

_____

_____

9. Two-thirds of the earth's coal (has, have) been used up. ___

_____

_____

Writing and Reading

Writing

You will be rewriting paragraphs in which there are agreement problems. Read the first one now and see if you can find the mistakes.

> Everyone on a ship are supposed to be friends. This is because the crew are always working together. Each of the sailors have a different job, but still work with the others. It is like a football team that have eleven players doing eleven jobs, but all works together for a common goal.

Practice

Rewrite the paragraph you just read correcting any errors in agreement.

1. _____
_____
_____
_____
_____
_____
_____

Now read another paragraph. See if you can find the mistakes.

> Neither the coach nor the players has the toughest job on a basketball court. It is the referee who wins my respect. The referee with his handy whistle are out there with ten tall players who looks as though they'd break him in half if he goes against them. Anyone who can stay out there for 48 minutes and keep their cool under such conditions have my sincere admiration.

Practice

Rewrite the paragraph you just read correcting any errors in agreement.

2. _____
_____
_____
_____
_____
_____
_____

Here's one more paragraph that needs help. Read it now.

Many people are animal lovers. But several doesn't like skunks. Why don't people like skunks? Do anyone ever hear of a skunk who try to hurt people? It isn't in the nature of a skunk to hurt even their worst enemy. Everyone know that skunks don't smell if they leave them alone. So if nobody hurt a skunk, a skunk won't bother them.

Practice

Rewrite the paragraph you just read correcting any errors in agreement.

3. _____
_____
_____
_____
_____
_____
_____

Reading

Read the story.

Once upon a time a pirate ship was wrecked on a small island far away from anywhere. Only a band of superstitious natives who believed in witches and devils lived on the island, so the pirate crew decided to take charge.

continued →

"That bunch is stupid," said a one-eyed pirate, "or else I'm the king of England."

"All natives are stupid," said the pirate captain. "We'll have to teach them how to work—for us! They'll be our slaves. This island will make a good kingdom for us."

So the captain put a crown of his best stolen jewels on his head and announced to the natives that he was their king.

Do this, do that! Get this, get that! The orders from the pirate king and his crew never stopped. So went the days and nights for several weeks, but the good life was not to last.

One night the king woke up from a nightmare. He had seen demons and phantoms dancing around his throne. They had long teeth like fangs and eyes that shot fire. They sang out with high, weird cries of warning: "Leave the island or you die!"

The king awoke trembling with fear. He sat up and was face to face with a skeleton. On its head sat the jeweled crown.

Then demons and phantoms just like those in his dream came dancing into his room. "Leave the island!" they sang in their high, weird voices. The king jumped out of bed and ran for the door. Standing in the doorway was a demon with a gigantic, hideous head. It raised a menacing finger and pointed at the king. "Now you die," it cried.

The king waited no longer. Forgetting his crown of jewels, he leaped out of a window. Once outside, the king was joined by the entire pirate crew. All of them were racing wildly for the ocean. Leaping into the water, they swam and swam and swam. How far they got, no one knows.

After the pirates were out of sight, the natives came out laughing and talking to each other. "Well, now we can put away those demon costumes and skeletons until the next time."

Practice

Answer each question by writing the letter of the correct answer.

4. What is this story about? _____
   a. How the pirates fooled the natives
   b. How the natives fooled the pirates
   c. How the pirates lived with the natives
5. Who first lived on the island? _____
   a. Pirates
   b. Witches and devils
   c. Natives
6. Who thought of making slaves out of the natives? _____
   a. The witch
   b. The captain
   c. The one-eyed pirate
7. Why did the captain think he could be king? _____
   a. He thought the natives were stupid.
   b. He thought the natives were afraid of his crew.
   c. He thought the natives liked him.

continued→

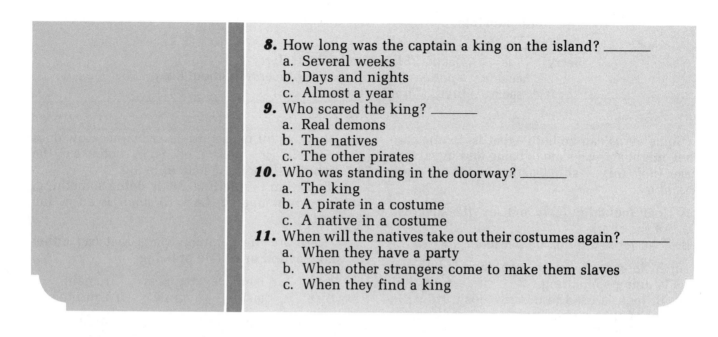

8. How long was the captain a king on the island? _____
   a. Several weeks
   b. Days and nights
   c. Almost a year
9. Who scared the king? _____
   a. Real demons
   b. The natives
   c. The other pirates
10. Who was standing in the doorway? _____
   a. The king
   b. A pirate in a costume
   c. A native in a costume
11. When will the natives take out their costumes again? _____
   a. When they have a party
   b. When other strangers come to make them slaves
   c. When they find a king

FA-5
Using Adjectives and Adverbs

Verbs That Show Action and a State of Being

Do you remember the difference between verbs that show action and those that show a state of being? Action verbs tell what the subject is doing.

Action verbs

Tony **chases** the captain. (Tony is chasing.)
Jackie **looks** at the clock. (Jackie is looking.)
They **suggest** that he stay home. (They are suggesting.)

Verbs that show a state of being have a meaning like *be*. They are used to describe or tell more about the subject. Three state-of-being verbs are *be, become,* and *seem.*

	State-of-being verbs	
Barry	**is**	sleepy. (*Sleepy* tells about *Barry*.)
Liz	**became**	a police officer. (*A police officer* tells about Liz.)
You	**seem**	tired. (*Tired* tells about *you*.)

Some verbs can be both—that is, in one case they might show a state of being and in another case they might show action. Look at these examples:

A. Joan **looked** quickly and saw the shadow of the shark.
B. Joan **looked** quick on her feet.

In A, *look* is an action verb. Joan is looking. She is **doing** something.

In B, *look* is used to describe Joan. How did she look? Quick on her feet. So in B, *look* shows a state of being.

Here are two more examples:

C. With after shave all over his face and neck, Jim **smells** good.
D. With his nose broken, Jim **smells** poorly.

In C, *smell* is used to describe Jim. How does he smell? He smells good. So in sentence C, the verb *smell* shows a state of being.

In D, Jim is smelling. He is **doing** something. So in sentence D, the verb *smell* is an action verb.

Here are the common verbs that can either show action or a state of being:

look	feel	appear	remain
turn	taste	grow	continue

For these verbs you have to pay careful attention to the meaning of the sentence in order to decide if the verb shows an action or a state of being.

Practice

Write *action* if the verb in the sentence shows an action. Write *state of being* if the verb shows a state of being.

1. Ms. Fox turned the handle of the door. _____

2. Ms. Fox turned pale. _____

3. The cake tasted good. _____

4. With a cold, no one can taste very well. _____

5. The patient appears strong. _____

6. The ghost mysteriously appeared in the doorway. _____

Adjective or Adverb?

The word that follows a state-of-being verb describes the subject. What kind of word describes or modifies a noun—an adjective or an adverb? An adjective modifies a noun. So, you can use an adjective after a state-of-being verb.

	Adjective	
Maria is	**happy.**	(*Happy* tells about *Maria*.)
Dick seems	**tired.**	(*Tired* tells about *Dick*.)
The flower smells	**sweet.**	(*Sweet* tells about *the flower*.)

 *Rule 1*

An adjective can be used after a state-of-being verb.

After an action verb, you should use an adverb. The adverb adds the meaning of "how" to the verb. Study these examples:

Adverb

She played **happily.**   (*Happily* tells **how** she played.)
They talked **quietly.**   (*Quietly* tells **how** they talked.)

 *Rule 2*

Use an adverb after an action verb.

Read these two examples:

    A. Jack was nice.   (state-of-being verb + adjective)
    B. Jack spoke nicely.   (action verb + adverb)

In A, *nice* tells what kind of person Jack is—it describes him. It is an adjective.
In B, *nicely* tells how Jack spoke. It is an adverb.
Read the next two sentences. Try to figure out which word correctly completes each sentence.

    C. The music seemed (soft, softly).
    D. Margie sang (soft, softly).

Soft is an adjective. Softly is an adverb.

Answer the next two questions by writing the letter of the correct answer.

7. What word should be used in C? _____
    a. *Soft*, because an adjective follows a state-of-being verb.
    b. *Softly*, because an adverb follows an action verb.

8. What word should be used in D? _____
    a. *Soft*, because it describes Margie.
    b. *Softly*, because it describes how Margie sang.

Practice

Rewrite each sentence using the correct word. The first word in ( ) is an adjective. The second word is an adverb.

9. The submarine ascended (quick, quickly) to the surface. ___
_____

10. Then it was (quick, quickly) to submerge. _____
_____

11. The torpedoes are very (accurate, accurately). _____

12. Most torpedoes can be shot very (accurate, accurately). ___
_____

13. The boat sailed (easy, easily) through the calm waters. ____
_____

Changing Adjectives into Adverbs

As you might have already noticed, many adverbs end in -ly. In fact, many adverbs are formed simply by adding -ly to an adjective.

Adjective	Adverb
She is **slow**.	She ran **slowly**.
Her voice is **beautiful**.	She sang **beautifully**.
They seemed **anxious**.	They called **anxiously**.

Adjective	Adverb
slow	slow**ly**
beautiful	beautiful**ly**
anxious	anxious**ly**

 **Rule 3**

With just a few exceptions, the "how" adverbs are made by adding *-ly* to an adjective.

The following is a list of the exceptions mentioned in **Rule 3**:

Adjective	Adverb
hard	hard
fast	fast
good	well

To be sure you understand **Rule 3**, write the adverb that can be made from each of these adjectives.

14. sweet _____

15. correct _____

16. fast _____

Sometimes you will have to change the spelling of the word before you add -ly. Do you remember the spelling rules for words that end in a consonant + y? You change the y to i and add the ending. Here are some examples:

crazy	crazily
lazy	lazily

For adjectives that end in -le, you just drop the e and add -y.

capable	capably
able	ably

Write the adverb for each of these adjectives.

17. handy _____

18. noble _____

Practice

For each sentence, an adjective appears below the blank. If the missing word should be an adjective, write the adjective. If it should be an adverb, change the adjective into an adverb and write the adverb. Look back at the rules if you need help.

19. Naval officers are _____ for their sailors.
(responsible)

continued ➡

20. Carlin remained _____ throughout the game.
(lucky)

21. The cat jumped _____ into its owner's lap.
(happy)

22. The cat seemed _____ to stay there.
(happy)

23. The submarine descended _____ to a great depth.
(sudden)

Good **and** Well

In written English, you must be careful about the way you use *good* and *well*. *Good* is an adjective and *well* is an adverb.

Write the correct word in each of the following sentences:

24. Mr. Carlin looked _____ in his new suit.

25. Agnes wrote _____ .

In 24, the verb *look* shows a state of being, so you should use the adjective *good*. *Write* is an action verb in 25, so you should use the adverb *well*.

Telling the difference between *good* and *well* is not difficult. However, you may get confused because *well* has another meaning. The word *well* can also be an adjective that means *in good health*. Look at this example:

Ms. Able asked, "How are you, Mr. Barry?"
"I am **well**, thank you," answered Mr. Barry.
"How are you?"
"I am **well**, too," answered Ms. Able.

Here *well* is an adjective, and it means the opposite of *sick*.

You won't get confused if you can remember these points:

- *Good* is an adjective and *well* is the adverb that goes with it.
- The other *well* is an adjective that means *in good health*.

Practice

Write either *good* or *well* to complete each sentence.

26. George felt _____ about playing chess.

27. He became _____ at chess after playing all year.

28. He played _____ because he practiced every day.

29. Mr. A asks, "What's the matter? Are you feeling sick?"

Ms. B answers, "No, I am feeling _____ ."

30. Mr. A asks, "How is your pitching arm today?"

Mr. B answers, "The arm feels _____ ."

More Practice

Answer the questions by writing the letter of the correct answer.

For each sentence, an adjective appears below the blank. If the missing word should be an adjective, write the adjective. If it should be an adverb, change the adjective into an adverb and write the adverb.

1. What should you use after a state-of-being verb? _____
   a. Adjective
   b. Adverb

2. Which statement is true? _____
   a. After an action verb, you can use either *good* or *well*.
   b. *Good* is an adjective and *well* is its adverb.
   c. *Good* is an adverb and *well* is its adjective.

3. The battleship cruised _____ into international waters.   (slow)

4. A plane stays _____ on its course due to good navigation.   (accurate)

5. Ms. Seversky quickly became _____ at running
       (good)
   the business when Mr. Green was ill.

6. A monster appeared _____ around the corner.
       (sudden)

7. The sick baby remained _____ all night long,
       (silent)
   but his mother waited _____ by his crib.
       (anxious)

8. I was sick, but now I am _____ .
       (well)

9. The doctor appeared _____ while Mr.
       (calm)
   Grimmins screamed _____ .
       (wild)

10. The dog walked _____ toward its master.
       (lazy)

Relative Clauses

What Is a Relative Clause?

Do you remember what a **clause** is? A clause is a group of words containing a subject and a verb within a sentence.

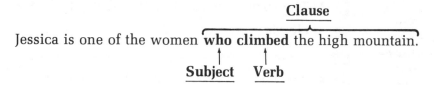

The clause you just read is called a **relative clause**. A relative clause is attached to a noun phrase by one of a few special pronouns:

who	that	where
whom	which	when
whose		

Here are some more examples of a relative clause. Notice that the pronoun in the relative clause is not always the subject of the clause.

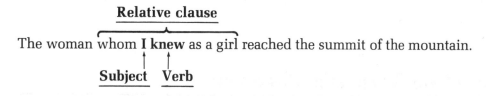

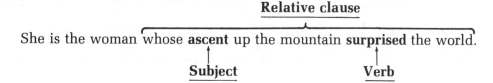

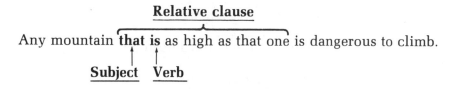

Remember:
1. Relative clauses start with one of the following pronouns:

who	that	where
whom	which	when
whose		

2. Relative clauses have a subject and a verb.

Practice

For each sentence, write the relative clause.

1. The jagged peak where the plane crashed was covered with clouds. _____

_____

2. No one remembers the time when I climbed a mountain.

_____

3. It is the baby who is making all the noise. _____

_____

4. The man whose hat I took by mistake was angry. _____

_____

Agreement in Relative Clauses

You have learned that a relative clause is like a sentence in that it has a subject and verb. This means that in the present tense the subject and the verb must agree with each other. Look at this example:

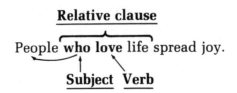

Relative clause

People **who love** life spread joy.

Subject   Verb

The pronoun *who* points back to *people*, which is a plural noun. So the verb *love* must be in the plural form.

Look at another example:

Relative clause

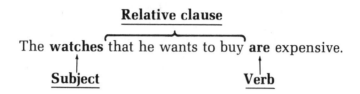

The watches that **he wants** to buy are expensive.

Subject   Verb

Of course the subject and verb of the sentence must also agree. The subject of a sentence will never be in the relative clause:

Relative clause

The **watches** that he wants to buy **are** expensive.

Subject   Verb

Practice

Rewrite each sentence using the correct verb forms.

5. The doctor who (sees, see) children (is, are) a pediatrician.

_____

6. The cliff that (goes, go) straight up (is, are) vertical. _____

_____

7. Several people whom Victor (knows, know) (has, have) been

robbed. _____

_____

8. The restaurant where they (likes, like) to eat (is, are) closing.

_____

Who, That, Where, and When

Look at examples A and B:

A. The clock struck thirteen. It was on the table.
B. The clock that was on the table struck thirteen.

A and B mean the same thing. The two sentences in A were added to make sentence B. This was done by turning the second sentence in A into a relative clause.

How could you go about adding these two sentences?

The woman is tired. She climbed the mountain.

First look for a word or phrase in the second sentence that points back to a noun or pronoun in the first sentence:

The **woman** is tired. **She** climbed the mountain.

Then change the second sentence into a relative clause by using one of the special pronouns:

She climbed the mountain.   **who** climbed the mountain

Last, put the relative clause after the noun it tells about:

The **woman who climbed the mountain** is tired.

Now look at the original two sentences and the sentence we just formed.

The woman is tired. She climbed the mountain.
The woman who climbed the mountain is tired.

....

How do you know which pronoun to use to start the relative clause? Let's take the case of the example you just read. The pronoun *who* is pointing back to *woman*.

The **woman who** climbed the mountain is tired.

The pronoun *who* is used for people or for animals that are given the qualities of people. Here are two more examples:

Jerry is a **girl who** is in my class.

I have a **dog who** thought she was a person.

The pronoun *that* is used for things. In casual talk it may be used for people, but in this lesson we will only use it for things:

The **pencil that** I bought yesterday broke in two.

Where must be used for "place" nouns:

The **store where** Mr. Fisher works is on fire.

And *when* must be used for "time" nouns:

I left at the very **moment when** Tim came into the room.

....

Look at some more examples of sentences that have been added by using relative clauses. Try to figure out why the specific pronoun was used to start the relative clause:

Sherry boosted me over the fence. It had just been painted.
Sherry boosted me over the fence that had just been painted.

Carmen knows a restaurant. We can get a milkshake there.
Carmen knows a restaurant where we can get a milkshake.

I like spring. At that time the flowers are in bloom.
I like spring when the flowers are in bloom.

Practice

Add each pair of sentences by turning the second sentence into a relative clause. Use the correct pronoun to start each clause: *who, that, where,* or *when.*

9. The girl told me not to feel discouraged. She won the race.

_____

10. The canoe is Mr. Old's. It has a hole in it. _____

_____

11. Mr. Perez waited at the store. We were to meet there. _____

_____

12. Jack hates the nighttime. At that time ghosts appear. _____

_____

Whose and Which

Use the pronoun *whose* when there is a possessive, like this:

> I know the woman. **Her record** is ten seconds.
> I know the woman **whose record** is ten seconds.

Do you see how *whose* takes the place of *her?* It can take the place of a noun in the possessive, too:

> I studied the old tree. **The tree's crown** was an apartment house for woodpeckers.
> I studied the old tree **whose crown** was an apartment house for woodpeckers.

Don't confuse *who* and *whose. Whose* is used when there is a possessive; *who* does not show possession.

There is no possession here.

> I saw the man **whose picture** is on the wall.
> I saw the man **who** took your picture.

This shows possession. The picture belongs to the man.

Some people also confuse *which* and *that.* You can use either *which* or *that* for things:

> I know the song. It is being played on the radio.
> I know the song **that** is being played on the radio.
> OR
> I know the song **which** is being played on the radio.

Use only *which* if it is the object of a preposition:

> Where is the money? I am to buy a diamond ring **with it**.
> Where is the money with **which** I am to buy a diamond ring?

Practice

Add each pair of sentences by turning the second sentence into a relative clause. Use the correct pronoun to start each clause: *who, whose, that,* or *which.*

13. I know a woman. Her sister survived an avalanche. _____

_____

14. It was a terrible avalanche. It buried a hundred houses. ___

_____

15. Where is that boy? His portable radio is so loud. _____

_____

16. We live on a plateau. It has an elevation of 8,000 feet. ___

_____

17. We all thought the movie about the woman was great. She catches a shark. _____

_____

18. Where is the book? I've heard so much about it. _____

_____

19. I learned all about the woman scientist. She discovered radium. _____

_____

Who and Whom

The pair of pronouns that causes most trouble is *who* and *whom.* The difference between *who* and *whom* is like the difference between *he* and *him* and *she* and *her.* One pronoun is used when it is the subject of the verb, and the other is used when it is the object of the verb. Use *who* when it is the subject of the verb:

Subject   Verb

The man stole the monkey. **He runs** a circus.

The man **who** runs a circus stole the monkey.

Use *whom* when it is an object of the verb or of a preposition:

Verb   Object

The man stole the monkey. You **caught him.**

The man **whom** you caught stole the monkey.

Preposition   Object

Who is the girl? You gave the book **to her.**

Who is the girl to **whom** you gave the book?

Remember:
1. Use *who* when it is the subject of a verb.
2. Use *whom* when it is an object.

Practice

Add each pair of sentences by turning the second sentence into a relative clause. Use either *who* or *whom* to start each clause.

20. My brother came home for Thanksgiving. He is in the army.

_____

21. Elaine doesn't like that pitcher. He always beats our team.

_____

22. Mickey is a pitcher. I like him. _____

_____

23. Ms. Peabody is a nice person. I would go out of my way for

her. _____

_____

24. Yesterday my sister called home. She lives in Paris. _____

_____

More Practice

Answer the questions by writing the letter of the correct answer.

1. How is a relative clause like a sentence? _____
   a. It is added to another sentence.
   b. It has a subject and an object.
   c. It has a subject and verb that agree.
2. What is the difference between *who* and *whom*? _____
   a. *Who* is used for the subject and *whom* for the object.
   b. *Who* is used in a relative clause and *whom* for the object of a preposition.
   c. *Who* is used for "time" nouns and *whom* for "place" nouns.

Add each pair of sentences by turning the second sentence into a relative clause. Each of the following pronouns should be used only once:

who	that	where
whom	which	when
whose		

3. Where is the car? I wanted to ride in it. _____

_____

continued

4. I wonder where the people went in the snowstorm. They were camping on the plateau. _____

_____

5. I wonder what happened to the people. We camped with them last summer. _____

_____

6. Marvin brought some news. It gave a boost to the weary climbers. _____

_____

7. We camped at a good location. Helicopters could find us here. _____

_____

8. I liked the story about the Indian. Her name was Blue Cloud.

_____

9. I was happy in the morning. At that time my friend came to visit. _____

_____

FA-7
Using Participial Phrases

Using the Present Participle in a Phrase

Do you remember what the present participle is? It is the form of a verb with the *-ing* ending.

Verb	Present participle
stop	stopping
take	taking
be	being

Write the present participle of the following verbs:

1. trespass _____

2. blame _____

3. hurry _____

4. hit _____

....

When a participle starts a phrase, that phrase is called a **participial phrase.** Some participial phrases begin with a present participle.

Participial phrase

Hurrying to get his lunch down, Mr. Epps got a stomachache.

Present participle

There is no subject in the participial phrase. So who is doing the hurrying in the sentence you just read? It's Mr. Epps. The subject of the present participle is the same as the subject of the main clause.

Here are two more examples of participial phrases beginning a sentence. Notice how the subject of the present participle is the subject of the main clause:

Present participle　　**Subject**

Being a farmer, **Harcourt** knew all about livestock.

Present participle　　**Subject**

Growing up on a farm, **Mary** learned a lot about livestock.

Remember:
1. Some participial phrases begin with a present participle—the *-ing* form of the verb.
2. The subject of the present participle is the same as the subject of the main clause.

Practice

For each sentence, write the participial phrase. Then next to it, write the subject of the present participle.

5. Waiting in the checkout line, I read a whole magazine.

_____　　_____

6. Flooding every spring, the river caused a lot of erosion.

_____　　_____

7. Traveling to the moon and back in two days, the Pacer set a record.

_____　　_____

Dangling Participles

If the subject of the main clause is **not** the subject of the participial phrase, the result is sometimes funny:

Stepping out of the airplane, the new airport sparkled in the sun.

HA! HA!

What is the subject of the main clause? It's *the new airport.* Is this the subject of the present participle? Is it the new airport that is stepping out of the airplane? Of course not. The writer does not mean that the airport stepped out of the airplane, but that is what the sentence says.

Mistakes like this are called **dangling participles** because the participial phrase is left dangling without a subject. Usually, dangling participles are easy to correct. All you have to do is supply the proper subject. For example, the sentence you read above could be corrected like this:

Stepping out of the airplane, Bert saw the new airport sparkling in the sun.

8. What is the subject of the present participle? _____
    a. the new airport   b. Bert   c. the sun

Read another sentence:

Thinking about the concert, my car ran out of gas.

9. As it is written, what does the sentence tell us? _____
    a. The car was thinking about the concert.
    b. The gas was thinking about the concert.
    c. The writer was thinking about the concert.

The pronoun *my* gives you a clue as to what the subject should be. You could easily correct the sentence by supplying the one subject that makes sense—*I.*

Thinking about the concert, I let my car run out of gas.

Practice

Rewrite each sentence so that you correct the dangling participle.

10. Growing angry at my boss, my work remained unfinished.

_____

11. Growing well in poor soil, I could cultivate rye on my land.

_____

12. Eating an ice-cream sundae, summer was on his mind. ___

_____

13. Needing a gift for Ms. Freeman, daisies were all she could

think of. _____

_____

Adding Sentences

In the last lesson you learned to add sentences like this:

The men were looking for gold. They found oil.
The men who found oil were looking for gold.

In that sentence we used a relative clause starting with the pronoun *who*. But there are often different ways to add the same sentences. Look at this example:

The men were looking for gold. They found oil.
Looking for gold, the men found oil.

Here the first sentence has been made into a participial phrase.

The example above was easy because the participial phrase was right there for us. All we had to do was move things around:

Participial phrase

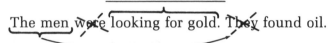

The men were looking for gold. They found oil.

However, the participial phrase won't always be there for you. Sometimes you have to make one up by changing a verb to the *-ing* form. Look at this example:

I felt sorry for Ms. Freeman. I bought her a gift.
Feeling sorry for Ms. Freeman, I bought her a gift.

Practice

Add each pair of sentences by using a participial phrase that begins with a present participle.

14. Mr. Pease drove downtown. He got a speeding ticket. _____

_____

15. Nickie has mechanical ability. She loves to fix things. _____

_____

16. I was stopping by the woods. I watched them fill up with snow. _____

_____

17. Andy cut across Mr. Bean's field. He was trespassing. _____

_____

Using the Past Participle in a Phrase

Another verb form is the past participle. It is the verb form that ends in *-ed* for regular verbs and has different forms for irregular verbs. For example, many irregular verbs end in *-en*.

Notice the different ways past participles are formed.

Verb	Past participle
stop	stopped
eat	eaten
drink	drunk
bake	baked
fall	fallen
buy	bought

Write the past participle of the following verbs:

18. walk _____

19. go _____

20. give _____

21. know _____

As with present participles, past participles are used to start participial phrases.

Participial phrase

Fallen to the ground, the alfalfa spoiled quickly.

Past participle

What is the subject of the past participle? It's *the alfalfa*. Once again, the subject of the participle is also the subject of the main clause.

Past participle   **Subject**

Fallen to the ground, **the alfalfa** spoiled quickly.

Look at another example:

Past participle   **Subject**

Destroyed by the bulldozer, **the woods** were overgrown with weeds.

Practice

For each sentence, write the participial phrase. Then next to it, write the subject of the past participle.

22. Baked in a pie, everything tastes good.

_____ _____

23. Seen from the air, the grove of peach trees looked like a box of jewels.

_____ _____

24. Robbed two times in one week, the bank manager hired two new guards.

_____ _____

More Dangling Participles

Past participles can also be left dangling when a writer doesn't stop to think. Here is an example:

Raised in Topeka, my education began in the home.

25. As this sentence is written, what does it tell us? _____
a. I was raised in Topeka.
b. I was raised in my home.
c. My education was raised in Topeka.

Just as you did with the present participles, you can correct these danglers by using an appropriate subject:

Raised in Topeka, I began my education in the home.

Practice

Rewrite each sentence so that you correct the dangling participle.

26. Started soon enough, I think conservation would have saved this river. _____

_____

27. Cultivated properly, farmers grow corn six feet tall. _____

_____

28. Raised in Texas, Nebraska is where the steers are shipped for slaughtering. _____

_____

More on Adding Sentences

As you can guess, two sentences can be added to make one sentence with a past participle. Study these examples:

I was shown how to do the work. I finished it quickly.
Shown how to do the work, I finished it quickly.

The child was lost in the morning. The child was found after lunch.
Lost in the morning, the child was found after lunch.

Practice

Add each pair of sentences by using a participial phrase that begins with a past participle.

29. Mrs. Lopes was driven to the store. Mrs. Lopes shopped all day. _____

_____

30. The boundary is marked by a stone fence. The boundary between the two farms is clear. _____

_____

continued

31. The dog was forgotten by its owner. The dog was waiting patiently. _____

_____

32. The house was drawn by Ernest. The house looked like a car. _____

_____

More Practice

For each sentence, write the participial phrase. Then next to it, write the subject of the participle.

Rewrite each sentence so that you correct the dangling participle.

Add each pair of sentences using a participial phrase.

1. Worrying about her son, Mrs. Callum called the police.

_____   _____

2. Tired from a day's work, Jack rested when he got home.

_____   _____

3. Using a tractor, a field of rye can be cut in half a day. _____

_____

4. Written on a typewriter, John wrote a story that I could read.

_____

5. Standing on the mountain, the sunset looked beautiful.

_____

6. Played by a good musician, I love that song. _____

_____

7. Mike was dreaming about participles. He didn't see the red light. _____

_____

8. Mike was given a ticket for it. He was angry at the light.

_____

9. The puppy was loved by its owner. The puppy was treated well. _____

_____

10. Mike thought he was going too fast. Mike slowed down.

_____

FA-8
Writing and Reading

Writing a Main Idea Paragraph with Supporting Details

Suppose you are writing about an opinion of yours, like this:

People should read advertising carefully.

1. What is it that you are mainly writing about?

————————

a. People   b. Reading   c. Advertising

The thing you are mainly writing about is your topic—advertising. And your main idea is what you are saying about the advertising:

People should read it carefully.

With that main idea you can write a whole paragraph. The rest of the sentences will grow out of that main idea. They will support the idea.

Why should people read advertising carefully? Write three or four answers to that question, and you will have a good main idea paragraph—a main idea and the supporting details.

Practice

Why must people read advertising carefully? Think of three reasons and write them.

2. ————————————————————

3. ————————————————————

4. ————————————————————

Write the main idea paragraph about advertising. Start by stating the main idea. Then write the three reasons you just wrote as supporting details so that they fit together to make a good paragraph.

5. ————————————————————

————————————————————

————————————————————

continued➡

_____
_____
_____

Now write a main idea paragraph. The first sentence should state your main idea, and the remaining sentences should give reasons that support your main idea. You can come up with your own main idea or use one of the following:
• People shouldn't drink heavily before driving.
• Drugs can be dangerous.
• Commercials can convince you to buy something.

6. _____
_____
_____
_____
_____
_____

More about Main Idea Paragraphs

You have seen paragraphs where the main idea is stated in a sentence in the paragraph. Some paragraphs have a main idea without stating it. For example, read the following paragraph:

> Have you ever seen a cartoon on TV or in the movies? It takes great imagination to make a cartoon because the characters are not real and the stories are not everyday events. Everything you see comes out of the minds of the authors who write what the characters say and the artists who actually create the characters. The result delights audiences of all ages. That is real art.

7. What is the topic of this paragraph? _____
   a. Imagination   b. Cartoons   c. Movies
8. Which of the following is the best main idea for this paragraph?

_____
   a. A great deal of imagination goes into making cartoons.
   b. Cartoons have interesting characters.
   c. Cartoons are very funny.

You have seen how supporting details can give reasons to support the main idea. They can also describe an example of the main idea. Read the following paragraph:

> A photographer can capture the immediate, on-the-spot experience. Suppose you are visiting friends. Their baby stands up and clumsily takes her first step. The parents beam with joy. Get that into a photo and you'll have a memorable picture for your photo album.

9. What is that paragraph mainly about? _____
   a. Babies   b. Taking photographs   c. Life

10. What is the best main idea of the paragraph? _____
   a. Photographs can capture important moments of life.
   b. Babies give joy to their parents.
   c. It is important to make your friends happy.

The paragraph about taking photographs illustrates one way of using supporting details. Instead of giving several reasons that support the main idea, it gives an example. The main idea is that photographs can capture important moments of life. The example of capturing a baby's first step is given to support the main idea.

Writing Another Main Idea Paragraph

This time you are to write an example that supports the main idea. For example, suppose your main idea is this:

Sometimes actions say more than words.

Now what you have to do is think of an example that illustrates this idea. Here is one possibility:

> Sometimes actions say more than words. Steve and Susan work in the same office. Steve was always boasting about how brave he would be if any emergency came up. Susan, on the other hand, was very quiet and shy. One day a fire broke out in the office. Steve panicked and didn't know what to do. It was Susan who called the fire department and got everyone out of the office to safety.

The example shows how Steve spoke of his bravery, but fell apart when he was put to the test. Susan, on the other hand, said little, but was able to cope with an emergency situation. These examples show that actions say more than words.

Practice

Write a main idea paragraph using an example to support the main idea. You can use one of the following main ideas or come up with one of your own:

- Smoking is bad for your health.
- There are many good shows on TV.
- Basketball players are overpaid.

11. _____

_____

_____

_____

_____

_____

Reading Main Idea Paragraphs

You have seen that a main idea may be handled in different ways:

1. State the main idea, then add several reasons that support it.
2. Instead of stating the main idea, give just the supporting details. The reader will then infer the main idea.
3. State the main idea, then add an example that illustrates it.

In each of the paragraphs that follow, look for the main idea; then look for the kinds of details that support the main idea. Read the first paragraph now.

Some baseball players think they're what makes the world go around, but Toby Taylor is just a nice guy. After yesterday's game with the Sox, I met him outside the dressing room. When I asked him for his autograph, he said, "Sure, kid." While he signed my scorecard, some other people came up with the same request. Toby sat down and started writing. He answered everyone's questions and told us how he was lucky to get into the big leagues. He wasn't stuck up at all.

Practice

Answer the questions by writing the letter of the correct answer.

12. What is the main idea of this paragraph? _____
   a. Some famous baseball players are stuck up.
   b. Toby Taylor likes to give people his autograph.
   c. Toby Taylor is a nice guy even though he is a famous baseball player.
13. How does the writer support the main idea? _____
   a. By giving an example
   b. By giving three or four reasons
   c. By stating the main idea

In your own words, write the example or the three or four reasons that support the main idea. (The answer to this depends on your answer to question 13.)

14. _____
_____
_____
_____
_____
_____

Now read another paragraph. Look for the main idea.

In this film the main character is a young woman played by an actress with no talent by the name of Cheryl Bates. This woman gets kidnapped by a monster and is carried off to a mountain cave. Suddenly she gets her head together and tricks the monster, who then falls off a cliff. This great story can be told in a few sentences, but it takes the movie *Monster Captive* two long hours. The special effects are terrible. They look as if they had been shot with a broken lens, and the sound quality is poor. If you do go to see this movie, my advice is to take a nap; at least the time will go faster that way.

Practice

Answer the questions by writing the letter of the correct answer.

15. What is the topic of this paragraph? _____
   a. The movie *Monster Captive*
   b. The audience
   c. Movies
16. What is the main idea of this paragraph? _____
   a. *Monster Captive* is an exciting movie.
   b. *Monster Captive* is a terrible movie.
   c. Sleeping in the movies is a good idea.
17. How does the writer support the main idea? _____
   a. By stating several reasons
   b. By giving an example
   c. By stating the main idea

Now read one more paragraph. Be sure to look for the main idea.

> The automobile is here to stay. Too many people live too far from public transportation to give up their cars in order to save gasoline. Many can't get to work or even to the store without their gas guzzler. They use their cars to go on vacations or to visit relatives who live hours away. Even the local movie theater is usually too far away to walk to. So the car may not be the best way to travel when it comes to saving fuel, but it is a necessity.

Practice

Answer the questions by writing the letter of the correct answer.

18. What is the topic of this paragraph? _____
    a. Vacations   b. The automobile   c. Transportation

19. What is the main idea of this paragraph? _____
    a. The automobile is here to stay.
    b. Too many people live too far from public transportation.
    c. People use cars to go on vacations.

20. How does the writer support the main idea? _____
    a. By stating several reasons
    b. By giving an example
    c. By stating the main idea

FA-9
Using Pronouns Correctly

Pronouns as Subjects and Objects

Each pronoun has several forms. One form of the pronoun is used when it is the subject of a verb. Another form of the pronoun is used when it is the object of a verb or preposition. Here are the forms:

Subject	Object	Subject	Object
I	me	we	us
she	her	they	them
he	him	who	whom

Practice

Rewrite the following sentences by substituting the correct pronoun for each underlined noun or noun phrase.

1. <u>Margie</u> is active in many clubs. _____

_____

2. No one thought that <u>Tom</u> would vote this year. _____

_____

3. Everyone likes <u>June and Fernando</u>. _____

_____

4. The speech made by <u>Mr. Cox</u> pleased the people. _____

_____

5. I wrote a song about <u>Mary and Joe</u>. _____

_____

Rewrite the following sentences by choosing the correct pronoun from the two in ( ).

6. John and (I, me) obey the rules. _____

_____

7. The dogs obey Sam and (she, her). _____

_____

8. Between you and (I, me), I don't like office politics. _____

_____

9. Sally and (he, him) drove across the country. _____

_____

10. The hit record is by John and (we, us). _____

_____

When Do You Use *Whom?*

Whom is the object form of the pronoun *who.* Look at the following example:

Subject
↓
Who called Joshua?

Object
↓
Joshua called **whom**?

Does "Joshua called whom?" sound a little strange to you? That's probably because the word order in questions with *whom* is usually turned around so that *whom* comes first:

Joshua called **whom**?

↓

Whom did Joshua call?

Whom also comes first in relative clauses:

Relative clause

Ms. King is a politician **whom** I know.

Object

Sometimes it's hard to know whether to use *who* or *whom*:

George is a secretary (who, whom) works for Ellen.

Should you choose *who* or *whom*? To decide,

make two sentences out of it, like this:

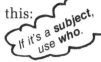

Subject

↓

George is a secretary. **He** works for Ellen.

Now what about:

George is a secretary (who, whom) Ellen knows.

Make two sentences out of it and you get:

*If it's an **object**, use **whom**.*   **Object**

↓

George is a secretary. Ellen knows **him**.

Whom is also used as the object of a preposition:

She is the candidate for **whom** I voted.

↑

Object of a preposition

Practice

Rewrite the following sentences by choosing the correct pronoun from the two in ( ). If the pronoun is the subject, use *who*. If the pronoun is the object, use *whom*.

11. I had lunch with a senator (who, whom) everyone admires. _____

12. I met with a reporter (who, whom) covered the presidential election. _____ _____

13. Jonah was the man (who, whom) the whale swallowed. ___ _____

14. (Who, Whom) did Juan ask for? _____ _____

15. (Who, Whom) took Juanita to the picnic? _____ _____

16. Karen is one person (who, whom) has contributed to the scouts. _____ _____

17. He is the one (who, whom) you met at the party. ___ _____

18. (Who, Whom) owns the Honda 450 that's in the parking lot? _____

continued →

19. Ms. Forsch is the one (who, whom) voted "Yes" on the highway issue. _____

_____

20. Mr. Blake is the one with (who, whom) I ride to work. ____

_____

Pronoun Reference

The words *refer* and *reference* mean "point to." If you refer to something, you point to it in some way. You might refer to a book. You might refer to what was said by someone. A pronoun refers too, like this:

When you see the pronoun *I* in a sentence, you know that it refers to the speaker.
When you see the pronoun *you* in a sentence, you know that it refers to the person spoken to.

Other pronouns refer to nouns or noun phrases in nearby phrases or sentences:

Harriet saw a lost dog. **It** looked hungry.

The woman was our doctor. We liked **her** a lot.

The senator asked my brothers to work on his campaign.

But **he** didn't meet with **them** until a month later.

In the last example there were two nouns and two pronouns, with each pronoun referring to one of the nouns. The problem in writing is to be sure that each pronoun refers clearly to only one noun or phrase. And the problem in reading is to be sure that you know which noun or phrase is referred to by each pronoun.

Practice

Rewrite the following sentences. Draw a line from each of the underlined pronouns to the noun or noun phrase referred to.

21. When Dorcas spoke on TV, <u>she</u> was very interesting. _____

_____

22. When the reporters stopped Dorcas outside the TV studio, <u>she</u> gave them <u>her</u> famous smile. _____

_____

continued

23. Some political candidates think <u>they</u> should be independent of <u>their</u> political party. _____

_____

24. The man to <u>whom</u> Amura spoke was <u>her</u> brother. _____

_____

Ambiguous Reference

When a pronoun refers to more than one noun or noun phrase, the pronoun is ambiguous. *Ambiguous* is pronounced **am BIG you us**. It is a fancy word, but it is not hard to understand. If a word can mean two or more things, it is called ambiguous. Read this example:

I liked the **play** in school.

Here the word **play** is ambiguous because it could mean games and fun or it could mean a story acted on the stage.

Pronouns can be ambiguous too. For example:

James told Ike that **he** was going to beat Charles.

Does *he* refer to *James* or to *Ike*? From the sentence alone, there is no way to tell. So *he* is ambiguous, and the whole sentence should be rewritten. If you want *he* to refer to *James,* you could rewrite the sentence this way:

James said to Ike, "**I** am going to beat Charles."

Here is another way to rewrite the sentence:

James thought Ike could beat Charles, and **he** said so to Ike.

Practice

Rewrite each of the following sentences so that the pronoun reference is not ambiguous.

25. Ms. Forster liked Ms. Hampton. She was a smart politician.

_____

_____

26. Once upon a time, Carlo and Chico were good friends. Then Carlo said to Chico that he was angry. _____

_____

continued ➡

27. After she started judo, Marcia realized that Dolores was athletic. _____

_____

28. The President told the senator that his activity in the legislature was important. _____

_____

29. The principal and vice-principal wanted to have a meeting with all the teachers. They knew they wanted to meet at once. _____

_____

30. After the people heard Paul and Mac on TV, they voted for the use of solar energy in schools. _____

_____

More Practice

Rewrite each sentence by choosing the correct pronoun.

1. The person (who, whom) works in a bank must be honest. _____

2. The person for (who, whom) I vote must be a good leader. _____

3. (Who, Whom) did you say you voted for? _____

4. She is the woman (who, whom) won the race. _____

5. I am the person (who, whom) you called last night. _____

Rewrite each of the following sentences and draw a line from each pronoun to the noun or noun phrase that it refers to.

6. The doctor whom Alice saw told her to stay home from school. _____

_____

7. Harold wanted Sylvia to go to the movies with him. _____

_____

8. Sylvia told Harold that she couldn't go this time, but she would love to go with him another time. _____

_____

continued

Rewrite the following sentences so that the pronoun references are not ambiguous.

9. Danny understood that Michael wasn't so dumb once he, too, learned about cars. _____

_____

10. The farmers grow peaches and apples because they are good. _____

_____

FA-10
More about Negatives

A Quick Review

What is the difference between A and B?

A. Bob is driving to Florida.
B. Bob is not driving to Florida.

Sentence A tells us something; it is positive.

And sentence B **denies** what sentence A tells; it is **negative**. And *not* is a negative word.

The word *not* comes after the first helping verb, and it denies what the verb part of the sentence tells us:

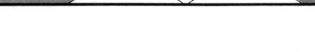

Helping verb   **Verb**
Gerald **had not tackled** the referee.
Negative

Helping verb   **Helping verb**   **Helping verb**   **Verb**
Janie **might not have been suspended** from the team.
Negative

Three helping verbs here.

Make the following sentence negative by adding *not* in the correct place.

The oil has been ruining the beaches all summer.

1. _____

_____

If the sentence has no helping verb and the verb is a form of *be*, you just add *not* after the form of *be*:

Bill **is not** happy.
Mr. Mothbatten **was not** at the concert.

Make the following sentence negative by adding *not* in the correct place.

The man was a prisoner.

2. _____

With other verbs, just add a form of *do* as the helping verb before you add *not*:

Positive: Martha wants to be manager of the team.
Negative: Martha **does not want** to be manager of the team.

Make the following sentence negative. *Be sure to use the correct verb forms.*

Nicki likes soccer.

3. _____

Do you remember how to turn a negative into a contraction? First you join *not* right to the helping verb, then you write just the n and the t with an apostrophe between them: **hadn't**.

Now you do it. Write the contractions for the following:

4. was not _____

5. should not _____

Remember the two spellings that don't follow the rule?

will not = won't
cannot = can't

Now that you've refreshed your memory on how to use *not* to make a sentence negative, let's take a look at some other ways of making a sentence negative.

Using *Never*

The word *never* is also used to make a sentence negative, but it is used a little differently than *not*. First, its meaning is not quite the same as *not*. Second, it isn't always added in the same place as *not*. Compare these examples:

A. Bobby has not disputed with the referee.
B. Bobby has never disputed with the referee.

6. In which sentence has Bobby "not disputed with the referee" for a **longer** amount of time?

_____

a. Sentence A   b. Sentence B

The negative *never* means "at no time in the past," so *b* is the right answer to 6.

Now notice something else about *never*:

She **never** will dispute a referee's call.
She will **never** dispute a referee's call.

As you can see, *never* can sometimes be put in different places in the same sentence, which is not the case with *not*.

Another important rule is that you do not have to add *do* as a helping verb when you use *never*:

*With **not** you need do.*

But you don't use do with never.

He played tackle on the football team.
He **did not** play tackle on the football team.
He **never** played tackle on the football team.

Don't try to make a contraction with *never* as you do with *not*. *Never* cannot be used in a contraction.

You can use a contraction here.

I can't find you.
I can never find you.

You cannot use a contraction here.

Practice

Rewrite each sentence as a negative two times. First, use *not* to form the negative. Second, use *never* to form the negative. If you wish, you may use a contraction where it is correct to do so.

7. The halfback fumbled the football. _____

_____

8. Maria thinks of summer when it snows. _____

_____

9. Some athletes have become wealthy. _____

_____

10. The orange trees will freeze in Miami. _____

_____

Using No

The negative *no* takes the place of a determiner:

This says there was a snake.

A snake was in her desk.
No snake was in her desk.

This one denies that there was a snake.

So it's easy to use *no*. Just put it in place of the determiner:

We traveled in **a** private jet.
We traveled in **no** private jet.

Sometimes the plural doesn't have a determiner:

I like sports cars.

So you just go ahead and put the *no* in front of the plural:

I like **no** sports cars.

Practice

Rewrite each sentence as a negative by using *no.*

11. Jenny flew a jet. _____

_____

12. Mike flies kites. _____

_____

13. Laura allowed pets in her apartment building. _____

_____

14. Rubber bands are extremely strong. _____

_____

15. Michelle heard the applause for her singing. _____

_____

56

Using *No One, Nobody, Nothing, None,* and *Nowhere*

The words *no one, nobody, nothing,* and *none* in the title of this section are negatives of other pronouns, and *nowhere* is the negative of an adverb. Here they all are:

Positive pronouns	**Negative pronouns**
everyone, someone, anyone	no one
everybody, somebody, anybody	nobody
everything, something, anything	nothing
any, some	none

Positive adverbs	**Negative adverb**
everywhere, somewhere, anywhere	nowhere

To make a sentence negative, replace the positive form with the negative form. Look at these examples:

Someone was playing Beethoven.
No one was playing Beethoven.

Anyone can play a guitar without lessons.
No one can play a guitar without lessons.

Something is wrong.
Nothing is wrong.

Who ate all the turkey? Ellen had **some**.
Who ate all the turkey? Ellen had **none**.

He plays soccer **somewhere** in Spain.
He plays soccer **nowhere** in Spain.

Practice

Rewrite each sentence as a negative by changing the positive pronoun or adverb into a negative one.

16. Adrienne knows something about English. _____

_____

17. Someone here knows how to play soccer. _____

_____

18. She went somewhere in Vermont to ski. _____

_____

19. Everything works when Josh fixes the car. _____

_____

20. Can anybody beat Victor in tennis? _____

_____

Double Negatives

Do you remember what a double negative is? It's saying *no* twice. There is a rule in English not to write double negatives. Here are some examples:

I **can't** go to **no** party.
Laura **wasn't** enjoying **none** of the shows.

To fix these, you just take away one of the negatives, like this:

I can't go to **the** party.
Laura **was** enjoying none of the shows.

Now we're going to look at sentences that are a little more complicated because they have more than one clause. There is a simple rule for such sentences.

Rule

Use no more than one negative in a clause.

Is this sentence OK?

Negative   Negative

Joey **didn't** like cranberry sauce, so **no one** offered him any.

The sentence is OK according to the rule. There are two negatives in the sentence, but there is only one negative in each clause.

Clause 1   **Clause 2**

Joey **didn't** like cranberry sauce, so **no one** offered him any.

But the following sentences are not OK because there is more than one negative in a single clause:

Both clauses are not OK.

Joey **didn't** like **no** cranberry sauce, so **no one** offered him **none**.
Laura **wasn't** going **nowhere**, so she **didn't** get dressed up.

The first clause is not OK.

The second clause is OK.

Practice

Rewrite each sentence by correcting any double negatives that appear in the same clause. If a sentence is OK as it is, write *OK*.

21. If you don't substitute alcohol for water in that experiment, you won't get the correct results. _____

_____

22. Kaplan never wrote nothing that was good English, and he wouldn't let anyone help him. _____

_____

23. No one went nowhere after the game because no one scored a goal. _____

_____

continued

24. Jerry didn't see nothing, so he didn't tell the detective nothing. _____

_____

25. I wouldn't say anything about Kaplan's English if I couldn't do no better than he. _____

_____

More Practice

Rewrite each sentence as a negative three times:
1. Use *not* to form the negative.
2. Use *never* to form the negative.
3. Use *no* to form the negative.
If you wish, you may use a contraction where it is correct to do so.

1. Adrienne liked the vegetables.

_____

_____

_____

2. A new car is worth the money you pay for it.

_____

_____

_____

Rewrite each sentence as a negative by changing the positive pronoun or adverb into a negative one.

3. Everyone was smiling when Jarvis played his guitar. _____

_____

4. I would like to go anywhere this weekend. _____

_____

5. She said something. _____

_____

continued ➔

Rewrite each sentence by correcting the double negatives.

6. I know there isn't no one home because no one answered when I called. _____

_____

7. Harold didn't have no fun at the zoo because there weren't no lions roaring. _____

_____

8. I don't want to do nothing tonight, so please don't call me.

_____

_____

FA-11
Making Comparisons

Comparative and Superlative Forms

As you know, an adjective has different forms to show comparisons.

A is **big**. B is **big**. C is **big**.
A is **bigger** than B. B is **bigger** than C.
A is the **biggest** of all.

These forms of adjectives are usually called **comparative and superlative**.

Comparative forms are -er: bigger, older, funnier, softer
          more: more wonderful, more musical
Superlative forms are -est: biggest, oldest, funniest
          most: most wonderful, most musical

The forms with *more* and *most* are used with adjectives of three or more syllables. The *-er* and *-est* endings are used with words of one syllable.

If an adjective has two syllables, you have to make a decision. Sometimes one form will sound better than another. Most two-syllable adjectives use *more* and *most*.

Adjective	Comparative	Superlative
urgent	more urgent	most urgent
special	more special	most special
brilliant	more brilliant	most brilliant

Adjectives that end in a consonant followed by *y* can use either form.

Adjective	Comparative	Superlative
funny	funnier	funniest
funny	more funny	most funny
healthy	healthier	healthiest
healthy	more healthy	most healthy

Generally, use the comparative form when you compare two things.

Mr. Freeman is **older** than Mr. Pierson.
That movie is **more terrible** than the one I saw last week.
John is the **taller** of the two men in the chorus.

Use the superlative form when you compare three or more things. Often you point out one thing from among the rest.

Mr. Freeman is the **oldest** man in the office.
That movie is the **most terrible** one I've ever seen.
Mike is the **tallest** of the three men at work.

Practice

There are mistakes in the adjective forms in some of these sentences. If you find a mistake, rewrite the sentence correcting the mistake. If the sentence is OK, just write OK.

1. Mr. Freeman is the oldest of the two singers. _____

2. Old Mr. Kirsh is the most older of all the singers. _____

3. Ms. Curzin is the interestingest speaker we've ever had. ____

4. Of the two of us, Elizabeth was the more courageous. _____

5. Of the two of us, she came to work earliest. _____

"How" Adverbs

"How" adverbs are mainly the *-ly* adverbs, like these:

wisely   maturely   naturally   lazily

Most of them are made by adding *-ly* to an adjective:

wise + ly   mature + ly   natural + ly

lazy + ly   *Change the y to i*

These adverbs can also be used to make comparisons. Here are some examples:

The major acted **more wisely** than the general. The sergeant acted **most courageously** in combat.

These *-ly* adverbs don't use the *-er* and *-est* endings—just *more* and *most*.

Some "how" adverbs don't end in *-ly*. A few of these will use *-er* and *-est* to make comparisons:

The ambulance drove **faster** than the bus.
No one works **harder** than Alvin.
Kelly ran **farthest**.

Practice

For each sentence, write the correct form of the adverb in ( ).

6. In defending the fort, Sergeant Pepper acted

_____ than Sergeant Salt.

(honorably)

7. But it was Private Mustard who acted _____

(honorably)

of all.

8. When the flag passed by, the senator saluted

_____ than anyone else.

(patriotically)

9. The private first class had to see the sergeant urgently; the

private second class had to see the sergeant urgently; but I

had to see the sergeant _____.

(urgently)

10. Of the three runners, Helen was the _____.

(fast)

11. Jack was _____ than Sarah.

(slow)

Special Words

There are some adjectives and adverbs that get mixed up and cause a little trouble. Look at these carefully:

Adjective	Comparative	Superlative	Adverb	Comparative	Superlative
bad	worse	worst	badly	worse	worst
good	better	best	well	better	best

Notice that the adjectives and adverbs are the same in the comparative and superlative forms. So the following words can be either adjective or adverb forms, depending on the sentence: *worse, worst, better,* and *best.*

Remember that adjectives are used after state-of-being verbs like these: *be, seem, feel, look,* and *appear.*

I **felt good** after breakfast.
She **seemed better** after she had eaten.
I **look best** when I dress up.

Use adverbs after action verbs:

I **write well**.
She **talks better** than I do.
Of all the women on the team, Laura **plays best**.

Practice

There are mistakes in some of the following sentences. If you find a mistake, rewrite the sentence correcting the mistake. If the sentence is OK, just write OK.

12. I acted bad; but he acted worst. _____

13. His actions seemed the worse of all those present. _____

14. Of all the players, she is the better. _____

15. The explosives worked so well that the bridge was completely destroyed. _____

16. The destruction caused by the fire was the worse we had seen. _____

Double Comparisons

Just as good writing avoids double negatives, it avoids double comparisons. For example:

Jerry plays checkers **more better** than Victor.
Keeping a dog out on a cold night is one of the **most unkindest** things anyone can do.

Correcting these sentences is easy. Just get rid of the extra comparison:

Jerry plays checkers ~~more~~ better than Victor.
Keeping a dog out on a cold night is one of the ~~most~~ unkindest things anyone can do.

Sometimes you will have a choice as to which comparison you want to keep.

Double Comparison: She is **more friendlier** than he is.
Correction 1: She is **friendlier** than he is.
Correction 2: She is **more friendly** than he is.

Practice

Rewrite each sentence correcting the double comparison.

17. Seeing the slain soldiers made him think that war was the most horriblest experience imaginable. _____

_____

_____

18. Hilda thought she was more maturer than Adrienne. _____

_____

19. That novel had the most awfulest writing imaginable. _____

_____

_____

20. After practicing, he wrote much more better than before.

_____

_____

More Practice

There are mistakes in some of the following sentences. If you find a mistake, rewrite the sentence correcting the mistake. If the sentence is OK, just write OK.

1. That cloth is more soft than this one. _____

_____

2. That's the wonderfulest book I ever read. _____

3. Of the four of us, Aggie was the prettier. _____

_____

4. Your dog is shorter than mine. _____

_____

5. Of the two of us, Elaine acted most wisely. _____

_____

6. Bobby was the most fast runner on the team. _____

_____

7. She swam badly, but you swam worse than she did. _____

_____

8. She felt badly, but you felt worst than she did. _____

_____

9. He looked well, but of the two she looked best. _____

_____

10. Of the two soldiers, he is best. _____

_____

Writing and Reading

What Is Cause and Effect?

A **cause** is anything that makes something happen. What happens is the **effect**.

Why did America drop an atomic bomb on Japan?

Here is one cause:

It wanted to end the war.

We can put the question and answer together and make a cause-and-effect sentence:

Cause	**Effect**
Because it wanted to end the war,	America dropped the bomb.

It's easy to recognize a cause-and-effect sentence when you see the word *because*. *Because* comes right before the cause.

Cause

I put on a coat **because** it got cold.

But not all cause-and-effect sentences have the word *because*. Then you have to use your common sense to figure out the cause and its effect.

Cause	**Effect**
After the sugar dissolved in the coffee,	the coffee became sweet .

The sugar dissolving in the coffee has the effect of the coffee becoming sweet.

Practice

For each sentence, write the cause and its effect.

1. She is a chemist, so she knows about acids.

Cause: _____

Effect: _____

2. With all of Susan's energy, she works all night.

Cause: _____

Effect: _____

continued

3. The sun and wind were strong, and the morning dew evaporated quickly.

Cause: _____

Effect: _____

4. Because I took aspirin and got some sleep, I felt better the next morning.

Cause: _____

Effect: _____

5. When the puppy licked my face, I couldn't resist buying him.

Cause: _____

Effect: _____

Reading Cause-and-Effect Paragraphs

Just as a sentence can have a cause and effect, a paragraph can show cause and effect. Read the following paragraph:

Why did Morgan make an error in counting the change for Helen? Was he trying to cheat her? That didn't seem possible, for they were old friends. The phone started to ring while he counted the money, and Morgan was expecting an important call. Evidently, Morgan was thinking more about the telephone than he was about the money.

Practice

Answer the questions by writing the letter of the correct answer.

6. In that paragraph, an effect was stated first. What was that effect? _____
   a. Morgan and Helen were old friends.
   b. Morgan was a cheater.
   c. Morgan made an error.

7. What was the cause in that paragraph? _____
   a. He was not thinking about the money.
   b. He was talking on the phone.
   c. He was trying to cheat.

8. One sentence in that paragraph is also a cause-and-effect sentence. Which sentence is that? _____
   a. Why did Morgan make an error in counting the change for Helen?
   b. That didn't seem possible, for they were old friends.
   c. Evidently, Morgan was thinking more about the telephone than he was about the money.

Some paragraphs will give several causes and ask you to infer, or figure out, the effect. The next paragraph is like this. Read it now.

> Dom had been good friends with Alex and Carmen until a month ago. Now they were acting strangely toward him. They wanted to have the office picnic on Sunday, when they knew he couldn't go. The three of them had planned to go to a concert together, but Alex and Carmen went without Dom. Carmen didn't even look at Dom in the hall this morning. Dom sat alone at lunch and stared at his onetime friends.

Practice

Answer the questions by writing the letter of the correct answer.

9. What likely effect has not been told to the reader? _____
   a. Dom is hurt and wonders why Alex and Carmen are no longer his friends.
   b. Dom likes Alex and Carmen.
   c. Dom is going to invite them to his birthday party.

10. What are all the causes for this effect? _____
   a. Dom had been good friends with Alex and Carmen.
   b. They wanted to have the picnic on Sunday, when they knew he couldn't go.
   c. They went to the concert without him.
   d. Carmen didn't look at Dom in the hall.
   e. Dom stared at them.

Read the following passage. Look for cause and effect as you read.

> It was not a normal winter. In January the temperature went down to zero and stayed there for a month. The water on the pond froze solid, right down to the bottom. I know, because I tried to drill a hole through it to go fishing. But it was too thick. Of course, it was swell for ice skating, and we played hockey until the end of February.
>
> Halfway through March, it thawed and presented us with a strange sight. Hundreds of dead fish were floating on the surface of the water. Yes, hundreds—Lila and I counted them. What happened? Had all of the ice skating harmed them? Then we realized that it must have been the ice. The water, frozen solid clear to the bottom, could provide no oxygen for the fish.

Practice

Answer the questions by writing the letter of the correct answer.

11. What caused the water to freeze to the bottom of the pond?

_____
   a. Zero temperatures
   b. Drilling to the bottom
   c. Going fishing

12. What were two effects of so much ice? (Write both letters.)

_____
   a. Good ice skating
   b. Playing hockey until the end of February
   c. Cold weather
   d. Catching fish

13. How did the writer and Lila know there were hundreds

of fish? _____
   a. They counted them.
   b. They caught them.
   c. They were told about them.

14. What caused the fish to die? _____
   a. The thaw
   b. Lack of oxygen
   c. So much ice skating

15. What is the main cause of the passage (the cause that started

everything else happening)? _____
   a. The lack of oxygen
   b. The ice
   c. The very cold weather

Writing Cause-and-Effect Paragraphs

You can write a cause-and-effect paragraph by starting with something that needs an explanation:

Why can prisoners go free on bond?

This states the effect. The rest of the paragraph should provide the causes. Look at this example:

> Why can prisoners go free on bond? No one is guilty until convicted in a trial. Therefore, until convicted, prisoners should be given their freedom—provided that there is reason to believe that they will show up for the trial. This is what a bond does. By putting up bond money, the prisoner will either show up for the trial or lose the money.

Here is another sentence stating an effect:

The water from the rain evaporated quickly.

Now, if you know what causes evaporation, you can write several sentences explaining what caused the water from the rain to evaporate quickly. You will then have a cause-and-effect paragraph.

Practice

Write a cause-and-effect paragraph. Start with the following sentence, which gives the effect:

As Julia entered the room, a shiver came over her.

Then choose three of the following "cause" sentences.

- She heard a movement in the corner, behind the curtain.
- She felt there was someone else in the room.
- She remembered that her roommate had the bad habit of leaving the back door unlocked.
- She should have heard the sounds of the TV.
- She tried the lights but they wouldn't go on.

Make sure that your paragraph reads smoothly.

16. _____

_____

_____

_____

_____

Choose two of the following "effect" sentences and use them to write two cause-and-effect paragraphs. Start each paragraph with the "effect" sentence. Then add two or three sentences that give causes.

- Detective Michael Burns did not investigate Sheila Thorne.
- Oil and water do not mix.
- George was afraid to ride the subway.
- Many countries of the Third World are anti-American.
- Many marriages are breaking up.

17. _____
_____
_____
_____
_____
_____
_____

18. _____
_____
_____
_____
_____
_____

FA-13
Capitalization and Conversation

Capitalization

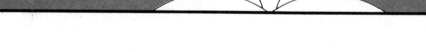

You know the important **capitalization** rules, so **capitalizing** words should not be much of a problem for you. There are some rules you haven't had yet, however, so this will be a good place to review what you know about using capital letters and to study what you do not know.

Capitalize First Words and Titles

 **Rule 1**

Capitalize the first word of every complete sentence.

You already know this rule. It applies to every type of sentence:

> **S**he is on a diet.
> **H**ow are you?
> **W**ow!

 **Rule 2**

Capitalize the first word of the salutation and complimentary close of a letter.

Here are some examples:

Dear Marge,	**D**ear Sir or Madam:
Very truly yours,	**S**incerely yours,

 **Rule 3**

Capitalize titles of books, songs, stories, and so on.

Study these examples:

> "The **S**tar **S**pangled **B**anner"
> *Moby **D**ick*
> "The **P**it and the **P**endulum"

You should note that not all the words in a title are capitalized. You do not capitalize small prepositions, but do capitalize prepositions of more than five letters:

> The first letter of the first word is always capitalized.

○ *The Call **of** the Wild*

"Coming **Through** the Rye"

You also do not capitalize the determiners *the, a,* and *an* unless they begin the title:

> *A Place in **the** Sun*

Do not capitalize *and, but, or, for, so,* and *yet* when they are used as conjunctions.

"The Pit **and** the Pendulum"

Practice

Rewrite these examples so that they are capitalized correctly.

This is a book title.

1. what are you talking about? _____
2. dear Henry, _____
3. gosh! _____
4. yours truly, _____
5. the old man and the sea _____

What Is "Proper"?

Here is a rule you know:

 **Rule 4**

Capitalize all proper nouns.

This rule is easy. But what's not always so easy is deciding what is a proper noun.

You should capitalize the following:

I. People

A.	Names:	Thelma Swift, George
B.	Titles with names:	Mrs., Rev., Ms.
C.	Words showing family relation-ships when used as names:	Dad, Aunt Sue

II. Places

A.	Streets:	Park Street, First Avenue
B.	Cities:	Detroit, San Diego
C.	States:	Texas, Ohio
D.	Specific parks:	Yellowstone National Park
E.	Bodies of water:	Hudson River, Indian Ocean

III. Periods of time

A.	Days:	Sunday, Wednesday
B.	Months: BUT NOT the seasons:	January, April summer, fall
C.	Holidays:	Memorial Day, Labor Day

IV. Special cases

Not all of the words in many of these special cases are capitalized. Use the same rules you used for titles.

A.	Points on the compass when they name regions:	Far East, the West, the South
B.	Important documents:	The Constitution, The Declaration of Independence
C.	Peoples, languages, and places:	French, American, Czechoslovakia
D.	Organizations, firms, schools:	Girl Scouts of America, Medical Supplies, Inc., Central High School
E.	Religions:	Catholic, Jewish
F.	Historic events:	Civil War, World War II
G.	Products with given names:	Heinz Catsup, Buick Skylark
H.	References to a supreme being:	God, the Lord, Allah

Practice

Rewrite each sentence so that it is capitalized correctly.

6. some chinese sailors got off the boat at the port in seattle.

_____

7. the declaration of independence is one of the most important documents in american history. _____

_____

8. last summer we drove south through the blue ridge mountains in virginia. _____

_____

9. if you are going to africa, the language to study is swahili.

_____

10. mr. olson works for the ford motor company, so at the end of the year he got a brand-new mustang at cost. _____

_____

_____

11. we asked aunt jane if she would celebrate washington's birthday with us by going to valley forge, where washington spent a cold winter during the revolutionary war. _____

_____

_____

Writing Conversation

What is the difference between sentences A and B?

    A. Allan said that his ankle was swollen.
    B. Allan said, "My ankle is swollen."

12. Do A and B mean the same thing? _____
    a. yes
    b. no

13. What is the difference between A and B? _____
    a. A reports what Allan said, but B gives the exact words.
    b. Only B tells us what Allan said.
    c. B is not punctuated correctly.

Sentences A and B are different ways of saying the same thing. Sentence B puts you right there—it gives you the exact words someone says. It is as if you are standing there listening. Sentence A, on the other hand, reports what Allan said. It's as if someone else is telling you what was said. This is why A is called an **indirect quotation**, whereas B is called a **direct quotation**.

Notice what changes are made when an indirect quotation is changed into a direct quotation:

Indirect quotation: The physician said that an X ray of my ankle was required.

Direct quotation: The physician said, "An X ray of your ankle is required."

Comma | **Capital** | **Pronouns** | **Verbs**

Quotation marks   **Quotation marks**

In the direct quotation:

1. A comma separates the words of the quotation from the rest of the sentence.
2. Quotation marks are put around the exact words that are spoken.
3. The first word spoken begins with a capital letter.
4. Pronouns are changed as necessary.
5. The tense of the verb is changed as necessary.

The verb refers to the past when the nurse was speaking.

Notice how the verb sometimes changes:

Indirect quotation: The nurse said that Ed need**ed** an operation.
Direct quotation: The nurse said, "Ed need**s** an operation."

The verb refers to the present time. The nurse is talking now.

Here I am telling what the nurse said.

Notice how the pronoun changes:

Indirect quotation: The nurse said that **I** needed an operation.
Direct quotation: The nurse said, "**You** need an operation."

Here the nurse was talking to me.

Now you try one. Rewrite the indirect quotation as a direct quotation.

14. Jack said that I should try out for the soccer team. _____

_____

If you want to change a direct quotation to an indirect quotation, you just do the opposite.

Direct quotation: Theodore screamed at me, "Close the door!"
Indirect quotation: Theodore screamed at me to close the door.

Practice

Rewrite each indirect quotation as a direct quotation. And rewrite each direct quotation as an indirect quotation.

15. Dominic said that his grandmother was ailing. _____

_____

16. The physician said that I'd have to go on a reducing diet.

_____

17. The nurse said, "A medical examination is required in order to make the soccer team." _____

_____

18. My doctor says, "Too much dieting is dangerous." _____

_____

continued

19. The reporter said that everything was peaceful in Bangkok.

_____

20. My driving instructor said that I drove very well. _____

_____

More Practice

Rewrite each sentence so that it is capitalized correctly.

1. michelle said, "my mother is puerto rican; my father is canadian; and I am american." _____

_____

2. in davis park on independence day, captain croft said, "my voyages across the atlantic and pacific oceans have taken me to many great lands, but there's no place like home." _____

_____

_____

3. in the civil war of the united states, the south and the north were at war. _____

_____

4. president lincoln signed the emancipation proclamation to free the slaves, but southern states like virginia refused to do so. _____

_____

_____

Rewrite each indirect quotation as a direct quotation. And rewrite each direct quotation as an indirect quotation.

5. Mary said that my brother was asking for me. _____

_____

6. The doctor said, "You need an operation." _____

_____

7. Burton said, "I am not an invalid." _____

_____

8. My boss said that I had to take a medical examination before I started work. _____

_____

9. Laura said, "I won't go to the party." _____

_____

Commas for Interruptions

An Interruption Means *Pause*

Whenever people talk, there are interruptions or breaks in the conversation. You've had that experience. Perhaps you are in the middle of a sentence and someone loses control and breaks in:

IKE: "This winter I'm going to go skiing in the—"
MIKE: "I'd love to go skiing this winter!"

We make certain interruptions when we write too. For example, you've probably come across the following kinds of interruptions:

> It'll cost a lot of money (a hundred dollars) to take up skiing.
> I want a book—any book really—that has some poetry in it.

The parentheses mark the interruption.

Here the dashes mark the interruption.

When you read a sentence out loud, you can hear the interruptions. First, there is a pause—a break—in the sentence:

Break   **Break**

It'll take a lot of money (a hundred dollars) to take up skiing.

After most pauses in a sentence, your voice goes down:

Pause, voice down

When Virginia started to read poetry, I left.

But when a pause is sudden—like a real interruption—the voice stays on the same level, waiting to continue:

Pause, voice stays level

I intend, if I have the ability, to become a great poet.

Of course, there is always a pause at the end of a sentence. This is the pause we mark with end punctuation, like a period.

Remember:
End punctuation marks a final pause.
A comma marks an interrupting pause.

Pauses at Quotation Marks

Read each of the following examples. Try to find out how many interrupting pauses are in each.

  A. Katie said, "Here I am!"
  B. "I read a fable about mice," said Walter.
  C. "This is a good book," said Wendy, "with lots of illustrations in the text."

How many interrupting pauses do you hear in each sentence? (Do **not** count the final pause that is marked by the period.) Write the number of interrupting pauses.

1. Sentence A: _____

2. Sentence B: _____

3. Sentence C: _____

Do NOT count the periods.

4. How are these pauses marked in the writing? (Write the letter of the correct answer.) _____
    a. by commas
    b. by periods
    c. by question marks

As you know, quotation marks are put around the exact words that someone has said. And of course you know that a pause is marked by the comma. So here is how we punctuate quotations:

1. Quotation marks start at the point where the exact words being quoted begin.
2. A comma is used for each interrupting pause.
3. End punctuation is followed by quotation marks.

Pause   Quotation marks

Aubrey asked, "Where is my diary?"

End punctuation

Did you notice that the start of a quotation is also the start of a sentence? This means that it needs a capital:

Capital letter

Aubrey asked, "Where is my diary?"

Sometimes the quoted words are interrupted by something like *he said* or *she said*. If this is an interruption in the middle of a sentence, the second part of the quoted material does not begin with a capital letter:

Interruption   Small letter

"Where," **Aubrey asked,** "is my diary?"

But if the second part of the quoted material begins a new sentence, you should use a capital letter:

Interruption   Capital letter

"Look out!" **cried Lolita.** "Here comes a car!"

The period here is a clue that one sentence has ended and another is going to begin.

Practice

Rewrite each sentence so that is is punctuated correctly.

5. I'd like to learn Spanish before I take my trip to Spain said Brenda _____

_____

6. do you want to know how to translate Spanish into English asked Sam _____

_____

7. yes answered Brenda that would be nice _____

_____

continued

8. I am Lolita Gonzalez said Lolita please call me Lo _____

_____

9. if I need help said Brenda maybe Lo will have time _____

_____

Appositives

An **appositive** is a word or phrase that further explains another word or word group, usually the one preceding it. Look at these examples of appositives:

Appositive

Ansel, my uncle, is a photographer.

Appositive

"The Cat and the Mouse," a fable, is in this book.

The words **my uncle** rename **Ansel**. They're two ways of saying the same thing. The same is true in the second sentence: *a fable* renames *"The Cat and the Mouse."* They are two different ways of saying the same thing.

So an appositive is different from a modifier in that it **says the same thing** as the word or phrase it is telling about. A modifier describes a word, but it does not rename that word.

Modifier   Noun

The **mountain photographs** by Ansel Adams are in the book.
(The word *mountain* describes the photographs.)

Appositive

He took **them, the photographs,** while he was vacationing in the Rockies.
(The words *the photographs* rename or mean the same thing as *them*.)

Practice

Rewrite each sentence so that it is punctuated correctly. Listen for pauses around the appositives.

10. Charmaine my sister is a poet _____

_____

11. I have read "Why Zoos Are for People" an essay _____

_____

continued ➡

12. Everyone takes English 3 "An Introduction to Literature"

_____

13. The coach said that Robin our shortstop wouldn't be able

to play _____

_____

Some appositives do not have commas around them because you don't pause when you read them.

Appositive	Appositive

My cousin Franklin is the author of **the essay "Modern Music."**

Now read this sentence:

Appositive	Appositive

Franklin, my cousin, is the author of **"Modern Music," an essay.**

But you need commas here.

There are two pauses in that sentence.

Remember:
If you hear pauses around an appositive, use commas.
If you don't hear a pause, don't use commas.

Practice

Rewrite each sentence that is incorrectly punctuated so that it is correct. If the sentence is OK as is, write OK. Use commas only when you hear a pause.

14. The fable "The Cat and the Mouse" is my favorite. _____

_____

15. Jackie my sister is a lawyer. _____

_____

16. My sister Jackie just won her first case. _____

_____

17. _Jaws_ my favorite book is also my favorite movie. _____

_____

More about Interruptions

Unlike appositives, many interruptions do not seem to be attached to anything. Some seem to be thrown into the middle of a sentence.

<u>**Comma**</u>   <u>**Interruption**</u>   <u>**Comma**</u>

My uncle, if anyone wants to know, is the author of a book.

The thing to do is this: **Read the sentence so it sounds natural;** if you hear a pause, use a comma.

In general, you should not have any interruptions between a subject and its verb.

<u>**Subject**</u>   <u>**Verb**</u>

The **storm hit** Amarillo at 6 P.M.

<u>**Interruption**</u>

Here is an interruption.

The storm, bringing three inches of water in two hours, **hit** Amarillo at 6 P.M.

There is nothing wrong with the second sentence. It follows all the rules. It is just a little harder to read because it puts the verb off for a long time.

Sometimes the verb can be put off a long time without pauses anywhere:

<u>**Interruption**</u>

The storm from San Antonio and the Gulf of Mexico **hit** Amarillo at 6 P.M.

Read the sentence. Listen to it. If you do not hear the pauses in it, do not use commas.

Practice

Rewrite each sentence that is incorrectly punctuated so that it is correct. If the sentence is OK as is, write *OK*.

18. Ms. Birney although she didn't know it was about to win a million dollars. _____

19. Dr. Jackal and Mr. Hood thinking they were too smart even for Batman called the police to report a murder. _____

20. A wind bringing warm air with gusts up to 30 miles an hour will announce a change in weather. _____

continued

21. No one not even my closest friend knows that I don't know a colon from a semicolon. _____

_____

_____

22. The baseball player Jackie Robinson a man of strong character died at the age of 53. _____

_____

_____

More Practice

Answer the questions by writing the letter of the correct answer.

1. What punctuation mark usually goes with an interruption? _____

    a. a comma   b. a period   c. a question mark

2. Which of the following has an appositive? _____
a. The doctor, a young woman in a Dodge, helped my father.
b. Call a doctor, for my father has fainted.
c. Our family doctor is Dr. Williams, who is also a poet.

Rewrite each sentence so that it is punctuated correctly. Some sentences will only need end punctuation. Other sentences will need commas and quotation marks.

Examples 3 and 4 are quotations.

3. Sarah asked what time is it _____

_____

4. I like you Mark said do you like me _____

_____

5. The textbook *Spanish for You* is in paperback _____

_____

6. *Spanish for You* the textbook is in paperback _____

_____

7. Someone perhaps Mr. Fletcher can remember when we last studied commas _____

_____

8. There is good acting in the movie *The Pawnbroker* which must be about 15 years old _____

_____

_____

9. My introduction to hurricanes if you call a roof down around your head an introduction took place in St. Petersburg, Florida _____

_____

_____

10. One way for you to avoid making mistakes in using commas is to read the sentence over carefully _____

_____

_____

FA-15
Using Verb Tenses

Being Consistent

The word *consistent* is often used to describe the way people perform:

A basketball player who shoots about 60 points in every game is *consistent*.
But a basketball player who shoots 30 points in one game and 90 points in the next game is *inconsistent*.

Being consistent in the way you write is important. Read paragraph A and B and see if you can identify the paragraph in which verb tenses change, or are inconsistent.

<table>
<tr><td>

A

Once upon a time there was a king who did not believe that his dukes and barons were loyal to him. They were courteous. They called him "Sir" and bowed before him, but did this prove they were loyal?

</td><td>

B

Once upon a time there was a king who will not believe that his dukes and barons are loyal to him. They were courteous. They call him "Sir" and bow before him, but does this prove they will be loyal?

</td></tr>
</table>

1. Which paragraph is *inconsistent* in its use of verb tenses? _____
   a. A   b. B   c. Neither

Good writers try to be consistent in their use of verb tenses, as in paragraph A. If they start out using a tense, they generally will keep to that tense.

Suppose the first sentence in a paragraph goes this way:

The baron and duke had taken a loyalty oath and had vowed allegiance to the king.

2. Which of the following goes best with that beginning? _____
   a. But the duke and his duchess were too urgent in their efforts to be loyal. If they heard anyone murmur a word against the king, they had the person thrown into a dungeon in their castle.
   b. But the duke and his duchess are too urgent in their efforts to be loyal. If they hear anyone murmur a word against the king, they have the person thrown into a dungeon in their castle.

3. Why is choice *a* the better answer for number 2? _____
   a. It is consistent in tense with the beginning.
   b. It is inconsistent in tense with the beginning.
   c. It continues the story.

In Conversation

When you write **conversation**, you may have people speaking in the present tense while you are writing in the past tense. Here is an example:

The king **said**, "That **is going** too far."
              ↑   ↑
        Past tense   **Present tense**

*Here, different verb tenses are **not** inconsistent.*

Sentences such as these are still consistent because the **writer is using the past tense** and the **speaker is using the present tense**. Here is another example:

  Past   **Past**   **Present**   **Present**
   ↓   ↓   ↓   ↓
Mark **fell** from the tree and **called** for help. "I **think** my leg **is** broken," he **said**.
                                    ↑
                                 Past

Practice

Complete the passage by writing the correct tense of each verb.

The King was unhappy. "Look, Duke," _____
                                              4. (says, said)
the King. "This _____ going too far."
                     5. (is, was)

"I _____ to show my allegiance to you, my lord,"
       6. (wish, wished)
_____ the Duke.
7. (says, said)

"It _____ not fair to the people who are in your
        8. (is, was)
dungeon," _____ the King. "Must it be a crime to
                 9. (says, said)
_____ your thoughts?"
10. (say, said)

In Compound Sentences

A **compound sentence** is one with two clauses joined by *and, but, or, for, so,* or *yet.* Some compound sentences do mix the present with the past or the future:

Ms. Crow **vows** to stop smoking, but **will** she?

　　　　　　Present　　　　　　　　　**Future**

Nick **had** the ambition of being a firefighter, but now he **is** a poet.

Past　　　　　　　　　　　　　　　　　　　　**Present**

Practice

Complete the passage by choosing the verb tense that makes the most sense.

"I am sorry," said the Duke, "and I _____ this
                                          11. (will not repeat,
                                                am not repeating)
mistake."

"That _____ good to know," said the King, "and
          12. (is, was)
I _____ you mean it."
   13. (hope, hoped)

In Adverb Clauses

Adverb clauses are clauses that start with adverb conjunctions like *if, because, since, although, when,* and some others:

John is nice
$\left\{\begin{array}{l} \text{if} \\ \text{because} \\ \text{since} \\ \text{although} \\ \text{when} \end{array}\right\}$
Mary is nice too.

In a sentence with an adverb clause, the two clauses are connected in meaning and the tenses must be consistent.

The general rule for adverb clauses is: **Past goes with past** and **present goes with present:**

Although she **has** a car, Gail **walks** to work.

       ↑   ↑
     __Present__   __Present__

Steve **rode** his bicycle to work when the weather **was** nice.

   ↑   ↑
 __Past__   __Past__

Practice

Complete the passage by writing the correct tense of each verb.

Because the King was a good man, he _____ to
                                      14. (announces, announced)

one and all the following: "When you are kind to others, you

_____ your King. I will be generous to you, if you
15. (please, pleased)

_____ be generous to all citizens of this kingdom,
16. (will, would)

including beggars."

After he had made this announcement, the King

_____ himself as a beggar, dirtying his face and
17. (dresses, dressed)

putting on shabby clothes, and _____ to the Duke's
                                         18. (goes, went)

castle.

The King knocked on the castle door and called out, "Have mercy! Have mercy!" But after he had knocked and called out

for several minutes, there _____ still no answer
                                   19. (is, was)

So he _____ out, "The King has spoken for
          20. (calls, called)

continued ➡

the beggars of the land. He will be generous to you, if you _____ help me."

21. (will, would)

As he was speaking, a window _____ and a

22. (opens, opened)

servant _____ garbage on him. Then a voice called

23. (throws, threw)

out, "Go away, beggar! Since the King is not here to see me disobey, I _____ not have to show you mercy."

24. (do, did)

The King had his horn hidden under his coat. When he blew the horn, all his soldiers _____ riding up.

25. (come, came)

"Duke!" shouted the King, as he _____ off his

26. (takes, took)

disguise. "I am the King. Although you _____

27. (know, knew)

my order, you still _____ not help a beggar who

28. (do, did)

asked for mercy; I cannot forgive you this time. Away to the dungeon with you!"

Is It a Fact?

The verb *be* has a special meaning when it is used with *if*, like this:

"**If** I **were** a beggar," said the King, . . .

The King isn't saying he once was a beggar. The King is saying: "Imagine for a minute that I am a beggar."

Ordinarily *were* is a plural form of *be* that means "past," as in "They were happy." But when used with *if*, *were* can be both singular and plural:

If the Duke **were** kind . . .
If the Duke and Duchess **were** kind . . .

When *be* and *if* are coupled, the phrase means "this is not a fact, but suppose for a minute that it is true." For example: "If the Duke were kind, he would have fed the beggar." But the Duke wasn't—so he didn't. So you see, it is **not** a fact that the Duke is kind.

Read the passage.

> One cold winter there was a thaw, and a cat and squirrel were talking.
> The cat said, "If I were a squirrel, I wouldn't work so hard all through the fall."
> The squirrel said, "If I were a cat, I would work a lot harder."

"If you were smart," the cat said, "you would be nice to the House People. Then they would feed you. And then you wouldn't have to work in the fall."

"If you were free like me," said the squirrel, "you would get your own food. Then you could lead your own life."

"I live my own life," said the cat. "I get the House People to do whatever I want."

"But you work very hard at it," said the squirrel.

"Ah!" said the cat. "But look at my bed. You must wish yours were as warm."

"Yes, but look at mine," answered the squirrel. "It is high in a tree, safe from those horrid children of the house."

That's how the cat and squirrel were arguing, each preferring its own way of life.

Practice

Read each statement. After each statement, write T if it is true or S if it is supposed.

29. The cat and squirrel were arguing. _____

30. The cat said the squirrel was smart. _____

31. The squirrel was really a cat. _____

32. The squirrel said the cat was free. _____

33. The cat does NOT think the squirrel's bed is warm. _____

More Practice

Read the following statements about using verb tenses. If the statement is true, write T. If it is false, write F.

1. In general, if you use a past tense in one sentence of a paragraph, you will use the present or future tense in the next sentence. _____

2. When coupled with *if*, the verb *were* is used sometimes to mean "not true." _____

3. In a sentence with compound clauses, the verb in each clause can be any tense so long as it makes sense. _____

Write the correct verb for each sentence.

4. Since Sadie is happy in Alaska, she (plans, planned) to stay there. _____

5. Because Hal was going to the store, he (takes, took) the shopping list. _____

6. Even if she (was, were) the best runner in the world, she would not be able to outrun a car. _____

7. If I (was, were) a king, I would rule with kindness.

_____

Writing and Reading

Reading a Sequence Paragraph

A paragraph is a way of grouping information. For example, **a main idea paragraph** will give an idea plus sentences that provide supporting information. **A cause-and-effect paragraph** will give a cause plus sentences giving the effects—or an effect plus sentences giving the cause or causes. **A sequence paragraph** is yet another way of giving information. It gives the reader a sequence of information. It tells us first this, then that, then something else, and so on, until the sequence is complete.

A **sequence** is a series of events in a special order. For example, here is a sequence paragraph you may be familiar with:

> For 8 ounces of spaghetti, use 3 quarts of water. Add 1 tablespoon of salt. Bring water to a boil. Add spaghetti and cook for 15 minutes, stirring frequently.

The paragraph gives the directions for cooking spaghetti—it is a recipe. Notice how it gives a step-by-step sequence for you to follow.

Look—this is a definition!

Practice

Answer the following questions on sequence. Write the letter of the correct answer.

1. What comes first in the sequence of cooking spaghetti? _____
   a. Turning on the stove
   b. Putting salt in the water
   c. Getting 3 quarts of water

2. What comes second in this sequence? _____
   a. Putting salt in the water
   b. Getting 3 quarts of water
   c. Bringing the water to a boil

3. Notice that the sentences in this recipe are all command sentences. They have no subject and start with a verb. What is the real subject of each of these sentences? _____
   a. I   b. You   c. He or she

Writing a Sequence Paragraph

A recipe is a step-by-step sequence. It tells what things to do and the order in which to do them. Do you know how to cook a soft-boiled egg? You will write a recipe telling how to do it.

Practice

Write your recipe in a paragraph that tells each step in the right order. Do these things:
(1) Start your paragraph with the word *First;*
(2) use command sentences;
(3) if you need help, read the **Help**.

Help

In case you're not sure you know how to boil an egg, here are some hints:

You will need: A pan, water to cover the egg, and a timer.

You will have to explain: When the water starts to boil, the egg will be soft-boiled in 2-3 minutes.

---

4. _____

_____

_____

_____

_____

_____

_____

_____

_____

_____

Reading More Sequence Paragraphs

Stories have many paragraphs in which their characters' actions are described in sequence, or in steps. Events in stories are also presented in this way. Where the characters go, what they do, and the order in which events happen all form part of a sequence. Read the following paragraph:

During World War I aviators flew those little aircraft that had two wings (biplanes). The plane was pushed out of its hangar before the aviator got into the cockpit. Then a mechanic started the engine by spinning the propeller by hand. The aviator pulled the goggles down over his eyes and, with a wave, took off down the grassy field.

Practice

Answer the questions by writing the letter of the correct answer.

5. What is the first thing that happened? _____
   a. The aviator got into the cockpit.
   b. The mechanic started the engine.
   c. The plane was pushed out of its hangar.

6. What is the second thing that happened? _____
   a. The aviator got into the cockpit.
   b. The aviator pulled the goggles over his eyes.
   c. The aviator took off.

7. Which of the following events is **not** in the correct sequence? _____
   a. The plane was pushed out of its hangar.
   b. The aviator got into the cockpit.
   c. The aviator pulled the goggles down over his eyes.
   d. The aviator took off.
   e. A mechanic started the engine.

Now read a longer passage that gives a sequence:

The snake, a cottonmouth, lifted its head over the shoulder of the highway and peered across the white concrete. Lowering its head, it began to move, zigzag, across the shoulder. When it reached halfway across the shoulder, there was a roar and rush of wind—a tractor-trailer raced by. The cottonmouth, a big one of almost five feet, stopped and waited. Cautiously lifting its head, it peered warily this way and that. Then it stared at its distant destination across the four lanes of concrete.

It lowered its head and started again. Apparently it was going to cross the highway regardless of the danger. Something across the way could not be resisted. On it went, gliding softly across the dark shoulder of the road like a silent underwater missile. Suddenly it stopped again. It was as if some radar in its head told it what to do, for a long black sedan raced by. Before continuing onward to the destination, the wary snake lifted its head and peered across the white road of sudden death.

Practice

Answer the questions by writing the letter of the correct answer.

8. What does this passage tell us? _____
   a. How snakes move
   b. How a snake moves across a highway
   c. What a cottonmouth does to get food

9. How far does the snake travel in the first paragraph? _____
   a. Halfway across the shoulder
   b. Halfway across the highway
   c. To the grass between the roads

continued

10. What does the snake do first after the truck races past?

_____
a. Hurries on its way
b. Turns around to go back
c. Looks around

11. What is the first thing that happens in the second paragraph? _____
a. The snake starts on its way.
b. The snake looks for danger.
c. The snake begins to glide softly across the shoulder.

12. When did the car race by? _____
a. When the snake started to glide on its way
b. When the snake stopped and looked
c. When the snake reached the highway

13. Why do you think there are two paragraphs in this passage? _____
a. A second paragraph starts when the car becomes the subject.
b. A second paragraph starts when the snake starts to move a second time.
c. A second paragraph starts because the snake is going to get hit by a car.

Writing More Sequence Paragraphs

Write a passage that shows sequence. Write about anything you want, but be sure to take your characters through all the necessary steps. If your sequence becomes _two different activities_, write _two paragraphs_.

If you have trouble thinking of something to write about, continue the story about the snake. For example, you might describe how the snake prevails, in spite of several near misses, and then reaches the far side of the highway.

Practice

Write a passage that shows sequence.

14. _____

_____

_____

_____

_____

_____

Sentence Puzzles

Different Compounds

Often you can make more than one compound out of the same two sentences. Let's start with:

My little next-door neighbor is a mischievous liar. He told his mother I was drunk last night.

The easy way to make a compound out of these sentences is to put a **coordinating conjunction plus a comma** between the sentences, like this:

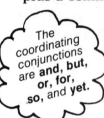

*The coordinating conjunctions are **and, but, or, for, so,** and **yet.***

My little next-door neighbor is a mischievous liar, **for** he told his mother I was drunk last night.

Since the subject of the second sentence is the same as the first, we can omit it and have just a **compound predicate:**

My little next-door neighbor is a mischievous liar **and** told his mother I was drunk last night.

No subject!

First rewrite the following pair of sentences to form a compound sentence. Use the conjunction *but*. Then rewrite the sentences to form a compound predicate.

Mr. Clark resembled a minister. He acted more like a gossip.

Compound sentence: **1.** _____
_____
_____

Compound predicate: **2.** _____
_____
_____

Some sentences can be turned into either a compound sentence or a sentence with a compound subject, like this:

A thief can be cunning. A liar can be cunning.

Compound sentence: A thief can be cunning, and a liar can be cunning.

Compound subject: A thief and a liar can be cunning.

Rewrite the following pair of sentences to form (1) a compound sentence and (2) a sentence with a compound subject:

The coffee tasted like mud. The tea tasted like mud.

Compound sentence: **3.** _____
_____
_____

Compound subject: **4.** _____
_____
_____

The next sentences can be turned into three kinds of compounds:

Last night Jack saw a car. Last night Jack bought a car.

Compound sentence: Last night Jack saw a car, **and** last night Jack bought a car.

Compound predicate: Last night Jack **saw a car** and **bought a car.**

Compound verb: Last night Jack **saw** and **bought** a car.

Two verbs

Two predicates

Write the following pair of sentences so they form (1) a compound sentence and (2) a sentence with a compound verb:

Sylvia worked in the library. Sylvia slept in the library.

Compound sentence: 5. _____
_____
_____

Compound verb: 6. _____
_____
_____

The last type of compound is a compound object:

The Japanese bombed Pearl Harbor. The Japanese bombed Wake Island.

Compound sentence: The Japanese bombed Pearl Harbor, **and** the Japanese bombed Wake Island.

Compound object: The Japanese bombed **Pearl Harbor** and **Wake Island.**

Rewrite the following pair of sentences so they form (1) a compound sentence and (2) a sentence with a compound object:

My progress fascinated the doctor. My progress fascinated the assistant.

Compound sentence: 7. _____
_____
_____

Compound object: 8. _____
_____
_____

Summary of Compound Types

Try to keep the following types of compounds in mind:

1. **Compound sentence:** The airline attendant helped the woman, and she thanked him.
2. **Compound subject:** A ping pong ball and a baseball are round.
3. **Compound predicate:** The movie pleased Carl and angered Julia.
4. **Compound verb:** The movie pleased and delighted Frederick.
5. **Compound object:** The movie pleased Carl and Melanie.

Practice

Each of the following groups of sentences can be turned into at least two of the five types of compounds. Rewrite each one to form two different compounds. Be sure to use each of the five types of compounds at least once.

Russia entered World War II in 1941. The U.S. entered World War II in 1941.

9. _____

10. _____

The U.S. dropped the atomic bomb in 1945. The U.S. defeated Japan in 1945.

11. _____

12. _____

Karl liked Einstein. Karl admired Einstein.

13. _____

14. _____

His frown concealed a kind heart. His frown concealed a funny streak.

15. _____

16. _____

Simone hated English. Simone loved French.

17. _____

18. _____

Relative Clauses and Adverb Clauses

There are two other common ways of combining two sentences. You can turn one of them into (1) a relative clause or (2) an adverb clause. Notice how the first example uses a relative clause:

To make a relative clause you must use **who, whom, whose,** or **that.**

That kid is like a mosquito. He frequently bugs me.

The kid **who** frequently bugs me is like a mosquito.

The next example shows an adverb clause:

The secretaries gossiped over their desks. I learned all about the assistant to the president.

When the secretaries gossiped over their desks, I learned all about the assistant to the president.

Some sentences can be turned into either a relative clause or an adverb clause:

The kid is like a mosquito. He bugs me.

Relative clause: The kid who bugs me is like a mosquito.
Adverb clause: The kid is like a mosquito when he bugs me.

Practice

Combine each of the following pairs of sentences by forming either an adverb clause or a relative clause.

19. The doctor arrived. It was almost too late. _____

_____

20. Scott kicked the ball too hard. It exploded! _____

_____

21. A ball should not have done that. It was brand new. _____

_____

22. The monkey was mischievous. It looked as dignified as a

Chinese scholar. _____

_____

23. They said the king had a billion dollars. He stole the billion

dollars from the people. _____

_____

Little Sentences in Big Sentences

Of course, instead of combining two sentences into one, we can also break long sentences into two shorter sentences. For example:

When I stopped smoking, I had no more colds.

1. I stopped smoking.   2. I had no more colds.

Read the following passage.

Tod Brady and James Scott played for the Vets. Tod was a pass receiver and kick returner. James was a kicker who could play quarterback if necessary. Both went to a little college in Alabama and were the best of friends. Since they had never been in a big city before, they shared an apartment and a car.

Practice

Rewrite the passage into shorter sentences. There are five long sentences in it now. When you rewrite it, there should be 11 shorter sentences.

24. _____

25. _____

26. _____

27. _____

28. _____

29. _____

continued

30. _____
31. _____
32. _____
33. _____
34. _____

More Practice

Combine the three sentences to make one long sentence:

Tod called. Tod told Kathy he had a date. Kathy felt sad.

1. _____
_____

Rewrite the long sentence into three short ones:

James liked the girl whom he met at the newspaper stand and vowed to speak to her.

2. _____
3. _____
4. _____

Rewrite the long sentence into two short ones:

That young musician whom I heard in Miami plays very well.

5. _____
6. _____

More Sentence Puzzles

Using Adjectives to Combine Sentences

Look at these sentences. How would you turn them into one sentence?

Guido is a dog. He is little.

The word **little** is an adjective, and an adjective can become a modifier, like this:

Little modifies dog.

It's an adjective because we can say littler and littlest.

Guido is a **little** dog.

We can combine sentences in this way whenever the verb **be** is followed by an adjective:

His mother gave Joel a punishment. The punishment **was harsh**.
His mother gave Joel a **harsh punishment**.

Practice

Combine each pair of sentences by making each adjective a modifier in the first sentence.

1. The spy smuggled the secret ashore. The spy was skillful.
_____

2. The yacht fascinated the girl. She was sensible. _____
_____

3. The yacht fascinated the girl. It was long and sleek. _____
_____

4. The outrigger raced through the waves. It was beautiful. ___
_____

5. The rogue tried to sell me an island. He was foolish. _____
_____

6. The climbers were tormented by harsh winds. They were weary. _____
_____

7. The waterfall fell 400 feet. The waterfall was amazing. ___
_____

Using Appositives to Combine Sentences

In lesson 14 you learned about appositives. Appositives are tied to a noun or noun phrase and are marked by commas or dashes. An appositive is a type of relative clause that has pauses:

Pause   **Pause**

I asked Mark, my cousin, to play tennis.

By using appositives, we can combine two sentences into one, like this:

One Eye leaped over the starboard bow. One Eye was the pirate.
One Eye, the pirate, leaped over the starboard bow.

Practice

Combine each pair of sentences by making an appositive.

8. Mr. Carlton robbed a bank. He is a piccolo player. _____
_____

9. I have a book on Mickey Mantle. He was a Yankee player.
_____

10. Holly Hollander waved from the gangplank. She is an actress. _____
_____

11. Tom's Corner has a population of 82. It is the best town in America. _____
_____

12. The yacht sailed past the reef. It was a 60-foot cruiser. ____
_____

Finding the Little Sentences in the Big Sentences

A sentence with an adjective or an appositive can be rewritten into two sentences:

The dangerous rogue was arrested.

(1) The rogue was arrested.   (2) The rogue was dangerous.

You can make three sentences out of the next one:

My uncle, the zookeeper, has a pet boa constrictor.

(1) My uncle is a zookeeper.   (2) My uncle has a boa constrictor.

(3) The boa constrictor is a pet.

Practice

Rewrite each of the following sentences into three sentences.

Finding a fish in his boot, Captain Paul, my uncle, suspected something fishy.

13. _____

14. _____

15. _____

The smaller boys love wrestling, and it is hard work.

16. _____

17. _____

18. _____

Beaten by the knight again, the dragon, a fire-breathing lizard, cried all night.

19. _____

20. _____

21. _____

More Practice

Combine the following sets of sentences by forming an appositive **and** a modifier.

1. Blackie sailed her yacht out into the winds. She was an experienced sailor. The winds were harsh. _____

_____

_____

2. Mr. Phelps spoke to the class. Mr. Phelps spoke harshly. He was the social studies teacher. _____

_____

_____

3. The storm blew giant waves. The storm was a hurricane. The storm was powerful. _____

_____

continued→

Read the following paragraph:

> The water ouzel, a thrushlike bird, lives in North America. Dipping into the water, it is a busy hunter of insects. Its nest, which is on the inside of a waterfall, is made of moss.

Rewrite the four sentences in the paragraph into seven sentences.

4. _____
5. _____
6. _____
7. _____
8. _____
9. _____
10. _____

FA-19
Sentence Rearrangements

Good Writing

Did you ever rearrange your room to make it look better? How about a sentence—did you ever rearrange a sentence to make it better? How can you rearrange a sentence? Try this one:

I'm joining the school orchestra.
The school orchestra is joining me.

You can't do that because it changes the meaning. Try this:

> I'm joining the orchestra **tomorrow**.
> **Tomorrow** I'm joining the orchestra.

That rearrangement is OK because it keeps the meaning.

Writers rearrange sentences usually for two reasons. Sometimes the change just sounds better. Sometimes the change makes a certain meaning stronger or clearer. It is these little things that make the difference between average writing and good writing.

"How" Adverbs

Nouns, verbs, and adjectives cannot be rearranged very easily. Their place in a sentence is pretty well fixed. But adverbs are different; they can be put in different places in a sentence:

The conductor conducts the orchestra **skillfully**.
The conductor **skillfully** conducts the orchestra.

The usual place for an adverb is at the end of a clause. So when it is there, it does not attract special attention to itself. But when the adverb comes earlier in a clause, it does attract special attention.

Rita looked up at me **slowly**.
Rita **slowly** looked up at me.

Practice

Rewrite each sentence by putting the adverb in a different place. (There is more than one way to rewrite each sentence.)

1. The President responded quickly to the questioning. _____

_____

2. The soprano and bass sang their duet softly. _____

_____

3. The duet was received warmly by the audience. _____

_____

Other Adverbs

You have worked with many other adverbs—mainly adverbs of "time" and "place":

John left **yesterday**.   **Time**

John left **Oakland**.   **Place**

John left **Oakland yesterday**.   **Place and time**

101

Of course, phrases also work just like these adverbs:

How   **Place**   **Time**

John left **in a hurry for the city at noon.**

Both the "how" and the "time" adverbs move around easily:

In a hurry John left for the city at noon.
At noon John left in a hurry for the city.

If you try rearranging the following sentence, some of the new sentences sound OK, but others sound strange.

How   **Place**   **Time**

The spy **calmly** flew the plane **to Denmark at night.**

Read these rearranged sentences. Notice how some sound OK, while others sound strange.

A. Calmly the spy flew the plane to Denmark at night.—**OK**
B. Calmly at night the spy flew the plane to Denmark.—**OK**
C. Calmly at night to Denmark the spy flew the plane.—**Strange**
D. At night the spy calmly flew the plane to Denmark.—**OK**
E. To Denmark the spy calmly flew the plane at night.—**OK**
F. The spy calmly at night to Denmark flew the plane.—**Strange**
G. The spy at night to Denmark flew the plane calmly.—**Strange**

Practice

Read the sentences carefully. How do they sound to you? If a sentence sounds OK, write *OK*; if it sounds strange, write *strange*.

4. She plays Chopin waltzes eagerly at home in the morning. _____

5. She eagerly plays Chopin waltzes at home in the morning. _____

6. At home in the morning eagerly she plays Chopin waltzes. _____

7. The orchestra played furiously during practice in school. _____

8. Furiously the orchestra during practice in school played. _____

9. During practice in school the orchestra played furiously. _____

10. Sometimes Nickie in the Met believed sincerely she would sing. _____

11. Sometimes Nickie sincerely believed she would sing in the Met. _____

12. In the Met sometimes sincerely Nickie believed she would sing. _____

Emphasis

If you bring out a certain meaning—or make that meaning stronger—you emphasize it. So by rearranging your adverbs, you can emphasize different meanings. For example, compare these:

She practiced eagerly every night at home.

Emphasize place: At home she practiced eagerly every night.
Emphasize time: Every night she practiced eagerly at home.
**Emphasize time
    and place:** Every night at home she practiced eagerly.

Practice

Rewrite each sentence and emphasize the time, place, or both, as directed.

I easily memorized a whole poem in an hour at home.

13. Emphasize place: _____

14. Emphasize time: _____

15. Emphasize both
    time and place: _____

She sang magnificently in Toronto last week.

16. Emphasize place: _____

17. Emphasize time: _____

He sang "Heartbreak Hotel" with feeling in the shower at night.

18. Emphasize place: _____

19. Emphasize time: _____

20. Emphasize both
    place and time: _____

Clauses

Adverb clauses can be rearranged too. The tricky thing about these clauses is the comma, although the general rule is fairly easy:

 Rule

In general, use a comma when the adverb clause comes before the main clause.

For example: **When the adverb clause comes before the main clause,** you should use a comma.
    The other side of this rule is: Usually you should not use a comma when the adverb clause comes after the main clause.

You will sometimes find an adverb clause stuck right in the middle
of a main clause, like this:

Pause   **Pause**

I thought, when I memorized the poem, I would like it more.

This is an interruption, so both pauses are marked with commas.

Practice

Rewrite those sen-
tences that are incor-
rect so that they are
punctuated correctly.
Write *OK* if the sen-
tence is correct.

21. When the opera star gestured magnificently from her tomb
I thought it was pretty silly. _____
_____
_____

22. It is magnificent music when she dies at the end of the
opera. _____
_____
_____

23. Even though I like music more than most people I find
opera a bit slow and too dramatic. _____
_____
_____

24. Even though they were supposed to be singing in English
I didn't understand one word of the opera. _____
_____
_____

25. Mozart was a child who before he learned to read wrote
wonderful music. _____
_____
_____

26. The snow even if it doesn't turn to rain will probably be
too wet for skiing. _____
_____
_____

27. I could conduct the orchestra if you want to know as well
as Bernstein. _____
_____
_____

More Practice

Rewrite each sentence by making the adverb clause an interruption in the main clause.

Answer the following questions by writing the letter of the correct answer.

1. After the Pirates won the series, the kids got Willie Stargell's autograph. _____
_____
_____

2. You'll like Westerns if you like opera. _____
_____
_____

3. The detective told us about the robbery long before you did.
_____
_____

4. Mrs. James can build a windmill if she gets the money. ____
_____
_____

5. What can you do by putting an adverb in a different place in the same sentence? _____
   a. Change the length of a sentence
   b. Change the meaning of a sentence
   c. Give the adverb emphasis

6. Which sentence gives an emphasis to time? _____
   a. Afterwards the girls softly sang a duet in a pizza parlor.
   b. Softly the girls sang a duet in a pizza parlor afterwards.
   c. In a pizza parlor the girls softly sang a duet afterwards.

7. Which sentence gives emphasis to place? _____
   a. Afterwards the girls softly sang a duet in a pizza parlor.
   b. Softly the girls sang a duet in a pizza parlor afterwards.
   c. In a pizza parlor the girls softly sang a duet afterwards.

Writing and Reading

Rewriting Paragraphs

The paragraphs you will read and rewrite in this lesson are the kinds you studied in lessons 8, 12, and 16: **main idea, cause and effect,** and **sequence.** Each paragraph can be improved by rewriting and rearranging the numbered sentences. Read the following paragraph:

1. Democracy is best for people. 2. It allows people to govern themselves. 3. Representatives of the people should make the laws. 4. The laws will reflect the needs of the people. 5. Most great civilizations have developed in countries that furthered individual freedom. 6. These countries were democratic. 7. It was in the republic of Athens that Western civilization had its initial and perhaps greatest period. 8. Athens was the first great democracy.

Practice

Rewrite the paragraph by doing the following:

1. Add sentences 1 and 2 so that sentence 2 is clearly the cause of sentence 1. _____

_____

_____

2. Add sentences 3 and 4 so that sentence 4 is the effect of sentence 3. (Hint: You can make sentence 3 an adverb clause or you can make one compound sentence.) _____

_____

_____

3. Combine sentences 5 and 6 by making *democratic* a modifier.

_____

_____

4. Add sentences 7 and 8 by making an appositive. _____

_____

_____

continued

Answer the questions by writing the letter of the correct answer.

5. What kind of paragraph have you written? _____
  a. A main idea paragraph
  b. A cause-and-effect paragraph
  c. A sequence paragraph

6. Why should representatives of the people make the laws?

_____
  a. So the country will become a democracy
  b. So the laws will be the laws of the people
  c. So civilization can develop

7. How did Athens further civilization? _____
  a. By having the first civilization
  b. By starting Western civilization
  c. By having the first democracy

Now read the next paragraph.

1. The people threw out the king finally. 2. They had reasons. 3. The reasons were numerous. 4. He cared only about his own desires. 5. He became a tyrant. 6. He had his army close down parliament. 7. The people no longer had representatives to speak for them. 8. The king loved opera. 9. He had many performances during his reign. 10. All opposition was silenced by his harsh rule for two years. 11. This king was not loved by the people. 12. He did not care for the people.

Practice

Rewrite the paragraph by doing the following:

8. For sentence 1, emphasize the adverb. _____

_____

_____

9. Combine sentences 2 and 3 by making *numerous* a modifier.

_____

_____

10. Add sentences 4 and 5 by turning 4 into a participial phrase.

_____

_____

11. Add sentences 6 and 7 by making a compound sentence.

_____

_____

continued ➔

12. Add sentences 8 and 9 by turning 8 into a participial phrase.

_____

_____

13. For sentence 10, emphasize the time adverb. _____

_____

_____

14. Add sentences 11 and 12 by making 12 a relative clause.

_____

_____

Answer the questions by writing the letter of the correct answer.

15. What kind of paragraph have you written? _____
   a. A main idea paragraph
   b. A cause-and-effect paragraph
   c. A sequence paragraph

16. What made the king a tyrant? _____
   a. He did not care about the desires of the people.
   b. He had the army run parliament.
   c. He was the people's only representative.

17. Look at your rewritten paragraph. Which sentence does not belong in this paragraph? Write that sentence here: _____

_____

_____

Read the following paragraph:

1. There came a sound through the bushes. 2. The sound was soft. 3. The female duck raised her head. 4. The younger ducks raised their heads. 5. She heard the noise again. 6. She took off. 7. The younger ducks took off after her. 8. The younger ducks spread their wings. 9. They made a great flapping noise. 10. Then two arms poked out of the bushes. 11. Then a rifle poked out of the bushes. 12. Bang! 13. Bang! 14. In midair the female duck stopped. 15. The female duck fell. 16. It tumbled lazily over and over. 17. She hit the pond with a splash. 18. The splash was hollow.

Practice

Rewrite the paragraph by doing the following:

18. For sentences 1 and 2, do two things: (a) Emphasize the place adverb in sentence 1 and (b) use sentence 2 to make a modifier in sentence 1. _____
_____
_____

19. Add sentences 3 and 4 so the action of sentence 3 is given before sentence 4. _____
_____
_____

20. Add sentences 5 and 6 by making sentence 5 an adverb clause meaning "time." _____
_____
_____

21. Add sentences 7, 8, and 9 as follows: (a) Make 7 a participial phrase; (b) then add 8 and 9 by making a compound predicate.
_____
_____

22. Add sentences 10 and 11 by making a compound subject.
_____
_____

23. Copy sentences 12 and 13 as they are. _____
_____
_____

24. Add sentences 14 and 15 by making a compound verb. ___
_____
_____

25. Add sentences 16, 17, and 18 as follows: (a) Make 16 a participial phrase; (b) then turn 18 into a modifier in 17. _____
_____
_____

continued

Answer the questions by writing the letter of the correct answer.

26. What kind of paragraph did you write? _____
   a. A main idea paragraph
   b. A cause-and-effect paragraph
   c. A sequence paragraph

27. What happened first? _____
   a. The duck raised her head.
   b. The younger ducks raised their heads.
   c. The soft sound came from the bushes.

28. When did the duck take off? _____
   a. The first time she heard the sound
   b. The second time she heard the sound
   c. When the hunter shot

29. When did the hunter shoot? _____
   a. Before the female duck took off
   b. Before the younger ducks took off
   c. After all the ducks took off

Answer Key

FA-1

1. Toast and jelly is not much of a lunch.
2. Toast and jelly are two foods I don't like.
3. Cake and donuts are good for dessert.
4. A cat and dog sleep in the sun on the porch.
5. Peaches and cream tastes good anytime.
6. A horse and buggy is coming down the street.
7. Dobrinsky or Carline is going on that dangerous mission.
8. The employer or the foreman inspects the new building each morning.
9. Only Jack or Mario has a chance of getting that job.
10. Neither candy nor ice cream has ever helped anyone lose weight.
11. Neither the cat nor the dogs know when to say no to food.
12. Either he or we are to get the prize.
13. Either the boys or Betty is knocking on the door.
14. Where is the architect who is responsible for the poor structure of this building?
15. There are many historical buildings in Trenton.
16. Where is the dome on the Capitol?
17. Near the river are the state buildings.
18. One of the writers has written about the local farmers.
19. The woman with the small baby in her arms is my wife.
20. People in that country choose their leaders by voting.

21.-24. Check with your teacher.

More Practice   ML: 9/11

1. Ice cream and Coke is not a good lunch!
2. There have been many problems in the world this year.
3. I knew one of the local farmers was growing corn for hogs.
4. The doctors talking with the tall nurse want help in room 804.
5. Neither I nor my sisters are going to be home for Thanksgiving.
6. Either my mother or some great Mexican cook has made these tamales.
7. The hamburger and two pizzas are ready to go.
8. After each game there are some fans asking for autographs.
9. Pizza and hamburgers are my favorite foods.
10. One of those men plays the guitar.
11. Only one art student out of ten wants to be an architect.

FA-2

1. The team is posing for its picture.
2. The typical crew on a pirate ship were criminals.
3. The public was amazed by the film on falling meteors.
4. The audience shows its amazement at the exhibit on solar energy.
5. The scout troop are pitching their tents.
6. The jazz band has a definite style.
7. The orchestra waits quietly for its conductor to appear.

8.-11. Check with your teacher.

12. Five more dollars gives the girl ten dollars.
13. A hundred pounds is not much for a fifteen-year-old boy.
14. Sixty-five years is an average lifetime.
15. Ten feet of fence is what I need.
16. Seven quarters are going into my piggy bank.
17. Some of the meteors burn up in space.
18. All of the meteor burns up in space.
19. The streets of the city are dangerous.
20. Half of the food is good.
21. Two-thirds of the students like rock music.
22. The men in the story were aliens from another planet.
23. Economics is her specialty.
24. His pants are too long.
25. The news is all bad.
26. The tweezers are on the table.
27. Her statistics do not agree with yours.

More Practice   ML: 8/10

1. The class is having its lunch in the park.
2. The family plan to save their money for a vacation.
3. Four inches is a lot to grow in one year.
4. One-third of the cake is yours.
5. Some of the fire fighters want to go on strike.
6. The scissors are in the sewing box.

Answer Key

7. Measles is not a serious disease these days.
8. Three weeks have gone by since I ordered that book.
9. Most of my time is spent on important matters.
10. The student committee have voted for their class president.

FA-3

1. c
2. c
3. b
4. c
5. b
6. a
7. Officer Crowell answers complaints every day, and many deal with mistreated children.
8. I have two younger brothers, and both look like me.
9. Few are able to do all that she can.
10. That group cut many records over the years, and several were very popular.
11. plays
12. has
*13. Everyone wants his or her children to be good students.
14. Two girls are on the baseball team, but neither thinks that she can be the team's best player.
15. Everything that fits me looks as if it is out of style.
*16. No one likes to get into an argument with his or her parents.

*17. Nobody in the police department has the authority to punish the criminal he or she arrests.
18. Ezra has given his speech before twenty other students, and everyone says he was good. In fact, they want him to speak again.
19. No one was surprised when Ms. Crane entered her plea of guilty; in fact, they would have been surprised if she didn't plead guilty.
*20. No one likes to pay for a parking ticket that he or she didn't deserve.
21. Everyone was helping Mr. Fritzky fix up his new house, and he appreciated their efforts.
22. Most of it was raw.
23. Most were good.
24. Three-fourths of the cake was gone.
25. Midge didn't think that any of the boys in school were her age.
26. Part was in Switzerland; part was in New York.

More Practice   ML: 7/9

1. Mr. Gordon liked everyone who was in his tenth grade health class; he just wished they would keep quiet.
2. Everyone in the class wasn't fond of rock music; Franklin knew several who were Beethoven fans.
3. Anyone who knows anything about law knows that anyone is innocent until proven guilty.
4. Maria ate one-eighth of the pie; the rest was left over.
5. Junk foods might taste good, but most are of no value.
6. Both are good swimmers.
*7. Everyone on this line wants his or her money back.
8. Everything I write in English turns out looking as if it is in Greek.
9. Two-thirds of the earth's coal has been used up.

*If you rewrote the sentence to avoid awkward wording, check with your teacher.

*If you rewrote the sentence to avoid awkward wording, check with your teacher.

Answer Key

FA-4

*1. Everyone on a ship is supposed to be friends. This is because the crew is always working together. Each of the sailors has a different job, but still works with the others. It is like a football team that has eleven players doing eleven jobs, but all work together for a common goal.

*2. Neither the coach nor the players have the toughest job on a basketball court. It is the referee who wins my respect. The referee with his handy whistle is out there with ten tall players who look as though they'd break him in half if he goes against them. Anyone who can stay out there for 48 minutes and keep his or her cool under such conditions has my sincere admiration.

*3. Many people are animal lovers. But several don't like skunks. Why don't people like skunks? Does anyone ever hear of a skunk who tries to hurt people? It isn't in the nature of a skunk to hurt even its worst enemy. Everyone knows that skunks don't smell if he or she leaves them alone. So if nobody hurts a skunk, a skunk won't bother him or her.

4. b
5. c
6. b
7. a
8. a
9. b
10. c
11. b

FA-5

1. action
2. state of being
3. state of being
4. action
5. state of being
6. action
7. a
8. b
9. The submarine ascended quickly to the surface.
10. Then it was quick to submerge.
11. The torpedoes are very accurate.
12. Most torpedoes can be shot very accurately.
13. The boat sailed easily through the calm waters.
14. sweetly
15. correctly
16. fast
17. handily
18. nobly
19. responsible
20. lucky
21. happily
22. happy
23. suddenly
24. good
25. well
26. good
27. good
28. well
29. well
30. good

More Practice   ML: 8/10

1. a
2. b
3. slowly
4. accurately
5. good
6. suddenly
7. silent, anxiously
8. well
9. calm, wildly
10. lazily

*You may have reworded some sentences to avoid the agreement problem or to avoid awkward wording. If you did, check with your teacher.

113

FA-6

1. where the plane crashed
2. when I climbed a mountain
3. who is making all the noise
4. whose hat I took by mistake
5. The doctor who sees children is a pediatrician.
6. The cliff that goes straight up is vertical.
7. Several people whom Victor knows have been robbed.
8. The restaurant where they like to eat is closing.
9. The girl who won the race told me not to feel discouraged.
10. The canoe that has a hole in it is Mr. Old's.
11. Mr. Perez waited at the store where we were to meet.
12. Jack hates the nighttime when ghosts appear.
13. I know a woman whose sister survived an avalanche.
14. It was a terrible avalanche that (which) buried a hundred houses.
15. Where is that boy whose portable radio is so loud?
16. We live on a plateau that (which) has an elevation of 8,000 feet.
17. We all thought the movie about the woman who catches a shark was great.
18. Where is the book about which I've heard so much?
19. I learned all about the woman scientist who discovered radium.
20. My brother who is in the army came home for Thanksgiving.
21. Elaine doesn't like that pitcher who always beats our team.
22. Mickey is a pitcher whom I like.
23. Ms. Peabody is a nice person for whom I would go out of my way.
24. Yesterday my sister who lives in Paris called home.

More Practice   ML: 7/9

1. c
2. a
3. Where is the car in which I wanted to ride?
4. I wonder where the people who were camping on the plateau went in the snowstorm.

5. I wonder what happened to the people with whom we camped last summer.
6. Marvin brought some news that gave a boost to the weary climbers.
7. We camped at a good location where helicopters could find us.
8. I liked the story about the Indian whose name was Blue Cloud.
9. I was happy in the morning when my friend came to visit.

FA-7

1. trespassing
2. blaming
3. hurrying
4. hitting
5. Waiting in the checkout line   I
6. Flooding every spring   the river
7. Traveling to the moon and back in two days   the Pacer
8. b
9. a
10. Growing angry at my boss, I left my work unfinished.
11. Growing well in poor soil, rye could be cultivated on my land.
12. Eating an ice-cream sundae, he had summer on his mind.
13. Needing a gift for Ms. Freeman, she could think only of daisies.
14. Driving downtown, Mr. Pease got a speeding ticket.
15. Having mechanical ability, Nickie loves to fix things.
16. Stopping by the woods, I watched them fill up with snow.
17. Cutting across Mr. Bean's field, Andy was trespassing.
18. walked
19. gone
20. given
21. known
22. Baked in a pie   everything
23. Seen from the air   the grove
24. Robbed two times in one week   the bank manager

25. c
26. Started soon enough, conservation would have saved this river.
27. Cultivated properly, corn is grown six feet tall.
28. Raised in Texas, the steers are shipped to Nebraska for slaughtering.
29. Driven to the store, Mrs. Lopes shopped all day.
30. Marked by a stone fence, the boundary between the two farms is clear.
31. Forgotten by its owner, the dog was waiting patiently.
32. Drawn by Ernest, the house looked like a car.

More Practice   ML: 8/10

1. Worrying about her son   Mrs. Callum
2. Tired from a day's work   Jack
*3. Using a tractor, I can cut a field of rye in half a day.
*4. Written on a typewriter, John's story could be read.
*5. Standing on the mountain, I looked at the beautiful sunset.
*6. Played by a good musician, that song is one that I love.
7. Dreaming about participles, Mike didn't see the red light.
8. Given a ticket for it, Mike was angry at the light.
9. Loved by its owner, the puppy was treated well.
10. Thinking he was going too fast, Mike slowed down.

FA-8

1. c
2.-6. Check with your teacher.
7. b
8. a
9. b
10. a
11. Check with your teacher.
12. c
13. a
*14. The example that supports the main idea is that Toby took the time to sign autographs for his fans.
15. a
16. b
17. a
18. b
19. a
20. a

---
*Your wording may be different. Check with your teacher.

---
*Your wording may be different. Check with your teacher.

FA-9

1. She is active in many clubs.
2. No one thought that he would vote this year.
3. Everyone likes them.
4. The speech made by him pleased the people.
5. I wrote a song about them.
6. John and I obey the rules.
7. The dogs obey Sam and her.
8. Between you and me, I don't like office politics.
9. Sally and he drove across the country.
10. The hit record is by John and us.
11. I had lunch with a senator whom everyone admires.
12. I met with a reporter who covered the presidential election.
13. Jonah was the man whom the whale swallowed.
14. Whom did Juan ask for?
15. Who took Juanita to the picnic?
16. Karen is one person who has contributed to the scouts.
17. He is the one whom you met at the party.
18. Who owns the Honda 450 that's in the parking lot?
19. Ms. Forsch is the one who voted "Yes" on the highway issue.
20. Mr. Blake is the one with whom I ride to work.
21. When Dorcas spoke on TV, she was very interesting.
22. When the reporters stopped Dorcas outside the TV studio, she gave them her famous smile.
23. Some political candidates think they should be independent of their political party.
24. The man to whom Amura spoke was her brother.
25.-30. Check with your teacher.

More Practice   ML: 8/10

1. The person who works in a bank must be honest.
2. The person for whom I vote must be a good leader.
3. Whom did you say you voted for?
4. She is the woman who won the race.
5. I am the person whom you called last night.
6. The doctor whom Alice saw told her to stay home from school.
7. Harold wanted Sylvia to go to the movies with him.
8. Sylvia told Harold that she couldn't go this time, but she would love to go with him another time.
9.-10. Check with your teacher.

FA-10

1. The oil has not been ruining the beaches all summer.
2. The man was not a prisoner.
3. Nicki does not like soccer.
4. wasn't
5. shouldn't
6. b
7. The halfback did not (didn't) fumble the football.
   The halfback never fumbled the football.
8. Maria does not (doesn't) think of summer when it snows.
   Maria never thinks of summer when it snows.
9. Some athletes have not (haven't) become wealthy.
   Some athletes never have become wealthy.
                    OR
   Some athletes have never become wealthy.

10. The orange trees will not (won't) freeze in Miami.

    The orange trees never will freeze in Miami.

    OR

    The orange trees will never freeze in Miami.
11. Jenny flew no jet.
12. Mike flies no kites.
13. Laura allowed no pets in her apartment building.
14. No rubber bands are extremely strong.
15. Michelle heard no applause for her singing.
16. Adrienne knows nothing about English.
17. No one here knows how to play soccer.
18. She went nowhere in Vermont to ski.
19. Nothing works when Josh fixes the car.
20. Can nobody beat Victor in tennis?
21. OK
22. Kaplan wrote nothing that was good English, and he wouldn't let anyone help him.
*23. No one went anywhere after the game because no one scored a goal.
24. Jerry didn't see anything, so he told the detective nothing.
*25. I wouldn't say anything about Kaplan's English if I couldn't do better than he.

More Practice   ML: 10/12
1. Adrienne did not like the vegetables.
   Adrienne never liked the vegetables.
   Adrienne liked no vegetables.
2. A new car is not worth the money you pay for it.
   A new car never is worth the money you pay for it.

   OR

   A new car is never worth the money you pay for it.
   No new car is worth the money you pay for it.
3. No one was smiling when Jarvis played his guitar.
4. I would like to go nowhere this weekend.
5. She said nothing.
*6. I know there isn't anyone home because no one answered when I called.
*7. Harold didn't have any fun at the zoo because there weren't any lions roaring.
*8. I don't want to do anything tonight, so please don't call me.

FA-11

1. Mr. Freeman is the older of the two singers.
2. Old Mr. Kirsh is the oldest of all the singers.
3. Ms. Curzin is the most interesting speaker we've ever had.
4. OK
5. Of the two of us, she came to work earlier.
6. more honorably
7. most honorably
8. more patriotically
9. most urgently
10. fastest
11. slower
12. I acted badly; but he acted worse.
13. His actions seemed the worst of all those present.
14. Of all the players, she is best.
15. OK
16. The destruction caused by the fire was the worst we had seen.
17. Seeing the slain soldiers made him think that war was the most horrible experience imaginable.
*18. Hilda thought she was more mature than Adrienne.
*19. That novel had the most awful writing imaginable.
20. After practicing, he wrote much better than before.

More Practice   ML: 8/10
1. That cloth is softer than this one.
2. That's the most wonderful book I ever read.
3. Of the four of us, Aggie was the prettiest.
4. OK
5. Of the two of us, Elaine acted more wisely.
6. Bobby was the fastest runner on the team.
7. OK
8. She felt bad, but you felt worse than she did.
9. He looked good, but of the two she looked better.
10. Of the two soldiers, he is better.

---

*There are other answers that are correct. Check with your teacher.

---

*Your wording may be different and still be correct. Check with your teacher.

FA-12

1. **Cause:** She is a chemist
   Effect: She knows about acids
2. **Cause:** Susan's energy
   Effect: She works all night
3. **Cause:** The sun and wind were strong
   Effect: The morning dew evaporated quickly
4. **Cause:** I took aspirin and got some sleep
   Effect: I felt better the next morning
5. **Cause:** The puppy licked my face
   Effect: I couldn't resist buying him
6. c
7. a
8. b
9. a
10. b, c, d
11. a
12. a, b
13. a
14. b
15. c
16.-18. Check with your teacher.

FA-13

1. What are you talking about?
2. Dear Henry,
3. Gosh!
4. Yours truly,
5. *The Old Man and the Sea*
6. Some Chinese sailors got off the boat at the port in Seattle.
7. The Declaration of Independence is one of the most important documents in American history.
8. Last summer we drove south through the Blue Ridge Mountains in Virginia.

9. If you are going to Africa, the language to study is Swahili.
10. Mr. Olson works for the Ford Motor Company, so at the end of the year he got a brand-new Mustang for cost.
11. We asked Aunt Jane if she would celebrate Washington's Birthday with us by going to Valley Forge, where Washington spent a cold winter during the Revolutionary War.
12. a
13. a
14. Jack said, "You should try out for the soccer team."
15. Dominic said, "My grandmother is ailing."
16. The physician said, "You have to go on a reducing diet."
17. The nurse said that a medical examination was required in order to make the soccer team.
18. My doctor says that too much dieting is dangerous.
19. The reporter said, "Everything is peaceful in Bangkok."
20. My driving instructor said, "You drive very well."

More Practice ML: 7/9

1. Michelle said, "My mother is Puerto Rican; my father is Canadian; and I am American."
2. In Davis Park on Independence Day, Captain Croft said, "My voyages across the Atlantic and Pacific Oceans have taken me to many great lands, but there's no place like home."
3. In the Civil War of the United States, the South and the North were at war.
4. President Lincoln signed the Emancipation Proclamation to free the slaves, but southern states like Virginia refused to do so.
5. Mary said, "Your brother is asking for you."
6. The doctor said that I needed an operation.
7. Burton said that he was not an invalid.
8. My boss said, "You have to take a medical examination before you start work."
9. Laura said that she wouldn't go to the party.

Answer Key

FA-14

1. 1
2. 1
3. 2
4. a
5. "I'd like to learn Spanish before I take my trip to Spain," said Brenda.
6. "Do you want to know how to translate Spanish into English?" asked Sam.
7. "Yes," answered Brenda, "that would be nice."
8. "I am Lolita Gonzalez," said Lolita. "Please call me Lo."
9. "If I need help," said Brenda, "maybe Lo will have time."
10. Charmaine, my sister, is a poet.
11. I have read "Why Zoos Are for People," an essay.
12. Everyone takes English 3, "An Introduction to Literature."
13. The coach said that Robin, our shortstop, wouldn't be able to play.
14. OK
15. Jackie, my sister, is a lawyer.
16. OK
17. *Jaws*, my favorite book, is also my favorite movie.
18. Ms. Birney, although she didn't know it, was about to win a million dollars.
19. Dr. Jackal and Mr. Hood, thinking they were too smart even for Batman, called the police to report a murder.
20. OK
21. No one, not even my closest friend, knows that I don't know a colon from a semicolon.
22. The baseball player Jackie Robinson, a man of strong character, died at the age of 53.

More Practice   ML: 8/10

1. a
2. a
3. Sarah asked, "What time is it?"
4. "I like you," Mark said. "Do you like me?"
5. The textbook *Spanish for You* is in paperback.
6. *Spanish for You*, the textbook, is in paperback.
7. Someone, perhaps Mr. Fletcher, can remember when we last studied commas.
8. There is good acting in the movie *The Pawnbroker*, which must be about 15 years old.

9. My introduction to hurricanes, if you call a roof down around your head an introduction, took place in St. Petersburg, Florida.
10. One way for you to avoid making mistakes in using commas is to read the sentence over carefully.

FA-15

1. b
2. a
3. a
4. said
5. is
6. wish OR wished
7. said
8. is
9. said
10. say
11. will not repeat
12. is
13. hope
14. announced
15. please
16. will
17. dressed
18. went
19. was
20. called
21. will
22. opened
23. threw
24. do
25. came
26. took
27. knew
28. did
29. T
30. S
31. S
32. S
33. T

More Practice   ML: 6/7

1. F
2. T
3. T
4. plans
5. took
6. were
7. were

Answer Key

FA-16

1. c
2. a
3. b
4. Your paragraph may be worded differently, but it should have the steps in this sequence: First, fill a pan with enough water to cover the egg. Turn the stove on high. When the water starts to boil, cook the egg for 2-3 minutes.
5. c
6. a
7. e
8. b
9. a
10. c
11. a
12. b
13. b
14. Check with your teacher.

FA-17

1. Mr. Clark resembled a minister, but he acted more like a gossip.
2. Mr. Clark resembled a minister but acted more like a gossip.
3. The coffee tasted like mud, and the tea tasted like mud.
4. The coffee and tea tasted like mud.
5. Sylvia worked in the library, and Sylvia slept in the library.
6. Sylvia worked and slept in the library.
7. My progress fascinated the doctor, and my progress fascinated the assistant.
8. My progress fascinated the doctor and the assistant.
9. Russia entered World War II in 1941, and the U.S. entered World War II in 1941.
10. Russia and the U.S. entered World War II in 1941.
11. The U.S. dropped the atomic bomb in 1945, and the U.S. defeated Japan in 1945.
12. The U.S. dropped the atomic bomb and defeated Japan in 1945.

    OR

    The U.S. dropped the atomic bomb in 1945 and defeated Japan.
13. Karl liked Einstein, and Karl admired Einstein.

14. Karl liked Einstein and admired Einstein.

    OR

    Karl liked and admired Einstein.
15. His frown concealed a kind heart, and his frown concealed a funny streak.
16. His frown concealed a kind heart and a funny streak.
17. Simone hated English, and Simone loved French.
18. Simone hated English and loved French.
19. When the doctor arrived, it was almost too late.

    OR

    The doctor arrived when it was almost too late.
20. When / Because } Scott kicked the ball too hard, it exploded!

    OR

    The ball exploded { because / when } Scott kicked it too hard.
21. A ball should not have done that because it was brand new.

    OR

    A ball that was brand new should not have done that.
22. The monkey that looked as dignified as a Chinese scholar was mischievous.
23. They said the king had a billion dollars that he stole from the people.
24. Tod Brady played for the Vets.
25. James Scott played for the Vets.
26. Tod was a pass receiver.
27. Tod was a kick returner.
28. James was a kicker.
29. James could play quarterback if necessary.
30. They both went to a small college in Alabama.
31. They were the best of friends.
32. They had never been in a big city before.
33. They shared an apartment.
34. They shared a car.

More Practice   ML: 5/6

1. When Tod called and told Kathy he had a date, Kathy felt sad.

    OR

    Tod called and told Kathy he had a date, so Kathy felt sad.
2. James liked the girl.
3. He met her at the newspaper stand.
4. He vowed to speak to her.
5. I heard that young musician in Miami.
6. The musician plays very well.

120

Answer Key

FA-18

1. The skillful spy smuggled the secret ashore.
2. The yacht fascinated the sensible girl.
3. The long and sleek yacht fascinated the girl.
4. The beautiful outrigger raced through the waves.
5. The foolish rogue tried to sell me an island.
6. The weary climbers were tormented by harsh winds.
7. The amazing waterfall fell 400 feet.
8. Mr. Carlton, a piccolo player, robbed a bank.
9. I have a book on Mickey Mantle, a Yankee player.
10. Holly Hollander, an actress, waved from the gangplank.
11. Tom's Corner, the best town in America, has a population of 82.
12. The yacht, a 60-foot cruiser, sailed past the reef.
13. Captain Paul found a fish in his boot.
14. Captain Paul is my uncle. } In any order
15. Captain Paul suspected something fishy.
16. The boys love wrestling.
17. They are smaller. } In any order
18. Wrestling is hard work.
19. The dragon was beaten by the knight again.
20. The dragon was a fire-breathing lizard. } In any order
21. The dragon cried all night.

More Practice   ML: 8/10

1. Blackie, an experienced sailor, sailed her yacht out into the harsh winds.
2. Mr. Phelps, the social studies teacher, spoke harshly to the class.
3. The powerful storm, a hurricane, blew giant waves.
4. The water ouzel lives in North America.
5. The water ouzel is a thrushlike bird.
6. It dips into the water.
7. It is a hunter of insects.
8. It is busy.
9. Its nest is on the inside of a waterfall.
10. Its nest is made of moss.

FA-19

1. The President quickly responded to the questioning.
   OR
   The President responded to the questioning quickly.
2. The soprano and bass softly sang their duet.
   OR
   The soprano and bass sang softly their duet.
3. The duet was warmly received by the audience.
   OR
   The duet was received by the audience warmly.
4. OK
5. OK
6. strange
7. OK
8. strange
9. OK
10. strange
11. OK
12. strange
13. At home I easily memorized a whole poem in an hour.
14. In an hour I easily memorized a whole poem at home.
15. In an hour at home, I easily memorized a whole poem.
16. In Toronto she sang magnificently last week.
17. Last week she sang magnificently in Toronto.
18. In the shower he sang "Heartbreak Hotel" with feeling at night.
19. At night he sang "Heartbreak Hotel" with feeling in the shower.
20. In the shower at night he sang "Heartbreak Hotel" with feeling.
21. When the opera star gestured magnificently from her tomb, I thought it was pretty silly.
22. OK
23. Even though I like music more than most people, I find opera a bit slow and too dramatic.
24. Even though they were supposed to be singing in English, I didn't understand one word of the opera.

25. Mozart was a child who, before he learned to read, wrote wonderful music.
26. The snow, even if it doesn't turn to rain, will probably be too wet for skiing.
27. I could conduct the orchestra, if you want to know, as well as Bernstein.

More Practice   ML: 6/7

1. The kids, after the Pirates won the series, got Willie Stargell's autograph.
                    OR
   The kids got, after the Pirates won the series, Willie Stargell's autograph.
2. You'll like, if you like opera, Westerns.
3. The detective told us, long before you did, about the robbery.
                    OR
   The detective, long before you did, told us about the robbery.
4. Mrs. James, if she gets the money, can build a windmill.
                    OR
   Mrs. James can build, if she gets the money, a windmill.
                    OR
   Mrs. James can, if she gets the money, build a windmill.
5. c
6. a
7. c

FA-20

1. Democracy is best for people $\begin{Bmatrix} \text{since} \\ \text{because} \\ \text{for} \end{Bmatrix}$ it allows people to govern themselves.
2. Representatives of the people should make the laws $\begin{Bmatrix} \text{and then} \\ \text{so} \\ \text{so that} \end{Bmatrix}$ the laws will reflect the needs of the people.
                    OR
   When representatives of the people make the laws, the laws reflect the needs of the people.
3. Most great civilizations have developed in democratic countries that furthered individual freedom.

4. It was in the republic of Athens, the first great democracy, that Western civilization had its initial and perhaps greatest period.
5. a
6. b
7. c
8. The people finally threw out the king.
                    OR
   Finally, the people threw out the king.
9. They had numerous reasons.
10. Caring only about his own desires, the king (or *he*) became a tyrant.
11. He had his army close down parliament, $\begin{Bmatrix} \text{and} \\ \text{so} \end{Bmatrix}$ the people no longer had representatives to speak for them.
12. Loving opera, the king (or *he*) had many performances during his reign.
13. For two years, all opposition was silenced by his harsh rule.
14. This king, who did not care for the people, was not loved by the people.
15. b
16. a
17. Loving opera, the king (or *he*) had many performances.
18. Through the bushes there came a soft sound.
19. $\begin{rcases} \text{After} \\ \text{When} \\ \text{Because} \end{rcases}$ the female duck raised her head, the younger ducks raised their heads.
                    OR
   The female duck raised her head $\begin{Bmatrix} \text{and then} \\ \text{before} \end{Bmatrix}$ the younger ducks raised their heads.
20. $\begin{rcases} \text{As soon as} \\ \text{When} \end{rcases}$ she heard the noise, she took off.
21. Taking off after her, the younger ducks spread their wings and made a great flapping noise.
22. Then two arms and a rifle poked out of the bushes.
23. Bang! Bang!
24. In midair the female duck stopped and fell.
25. Tumbling lazily over and over, she hit the pond with a hollow splash.
26. c
27. c
28. b
29. c

Facts are true statements or true pieces of information. When you read, you often read in search of certain facts. When you listen, you listen for facts too. Read the following paragraphs. Then answer the questions using some facts from the paragraphs.

On some nights the moon looks like a shining silver ball. On other nights, it seems to be only a slice of light. Sometimes when you look up at a rising full moon, it seems much larger just above the horizon than it does when it is overhead. Although the way that we look at it makes the moon appear large or small, we know that the moon's size always stays the same.

Only one side of the moon is ever completely visible to us on earth. This side is covered with many deep holes called craters. Many craters are several miles wide. The moon also has many cliffs and jagged mountains. The highest mountains have peaks of 26,000 feet or higher.

---

1. The moon seems larger when it is just above the _____ than it does when it is overhead.
2. The moon's size always stays the _____ .
3. Deep holes on the moon are called _____ .

Assignment: Use as many of the following words as you can to write an article that contains many facts.

architect	durable	foundation	local
architecture	employee	historical	quarry
asphalt	employer	hoist	site
derrick	erect	inspection	smash
dome	foreman	litter	structure

FA-2 Sequence

Events often happen in a certain order, or **sequence**. Sometimes authors use words such as *before*, *after*, *earlier*, and *then* in order to call attention to the sequence. Read the following paragraphs. Then answer the questions.

Irrigation is the watering of plants by artificial, or man-made ways. Without irrigation there could be no agriculture in dry places, because irrigation supplies water to farm crops.

Water is led from rivers and streams to farms that may be hundreds of miles away. Dams are built to hold back water in great man-made lakes call reservoirs. Most of the water taken to farmlands in the United States and Canada is run to the farms through open waterways called ditches, which are dug in the ground. The main ditch takes the water from the reservoirs to the farms. Smaller ditches leave the main ditch at regular places and then take the water to the fields.

In what sequence is water led from the rivers and streams to the crops? Put the sentences below in order by numbering them from 1 to 3.
a._____   The main ditch takes water from the reservoir to the farms.
b._____   Dams are built to hold back water in great man-made lakes.
c._____   Small ditches leave the main ditch at regular places and take the water to the fields.

Assignment: Write a few paragraphs in which events happen in a certain order. After you write the paragraphs, list the events in the order in which they took place. Use as many of the following words as possible when you do your writing.

alien	definite	hydrogen	positive
amazement	diameter	indicate	purify
astronomy	element	meteor	solar
carbon	exploration	nitrogen	substance
comparison	genuine	ponder	typical

FA-3 Main Idea

The **main idea** of a paragraph is the most important point in the paragraph. Sometimes a single sentence in the paragraph gives you the main idea. Other times, the main idea is not directly stated and you have to read the paragraph very carefully to find out the most important point. Read the following paragraph. Then choose the main idea.

> Shortly before noon on March 6, 1970, an elegant four-story town house in the heart of Greenwich Village was completely blown up and leveled by explosions and fire. Neighbors who were nearby said that they heard three huge explosions, and then the building started to burn. The house was so completely in ruins that it wasn't until a week later that the police found that three people had been killed in the explosions.

Which of the following states the main idea?
1. The huge explosions and fire took place on March 6, 1970.
2. Three people were killed in a fire and explosions that leveled a four-story town house.
3. The house was located in Greenwich Village in New York City.

Assignment: Look at the words below. Write a short paragraph using as many of them as you can. Then write the main idea of your paragraph, or what your paragraph is about. The main idea can be stated with one or two sentences from the paragraph.

argument	criminal	inherit	punishment
authority	estate	judgment	responsibility
complaint	federal	jury	superior
condemn	guilty	legal	supreme
counsel	identify	plea	swore

FA-4 Context Clues

When you read, you sometimes come to a word you do not know. When this happens, you can often figure out the meaning of the word from the other words around it, or its context. Sometimes, but not always, the author will help you by including such signal words as *that is, which is, in other words,* or *means.* Other times, authors might give examples to explain the meaning of new words.

Read the following three paragraphs. Then complete the chart below.

> According to Greek mythology, that is, the legends or stories of the ancient Greeks, Helen of Troy was the most beautiful woman in the world.
>
> Paris was the son of the King of Troy. He fell in love with Helen, kidnapped her, or stole her by force, and brought her to Troy.
>
> It was not proper for Paris to have done this, for Helen was already married to Menelaus, the King of Sparta. When Paris carried Helen off to Troy, Menelaus gathered a large Greek army and attacked Troy. The war was one of the fiercest conflicts, or battles of ancient times.

Words	Signals	Meaning
1. mythology		
2. kidnapped		
3. conflict		

Assignment: Write a paragraph that uses at least seven of the words below. Use other words in your paragraph to tell the meaning of each of the seven words. You may use signal words if it makes your paragraph clearer.

beware	fang	nightmare	tomb
cemetery	gigantic	phantom	torment
curse	hideous	ravenous	twitch
demon	menace	skeleton	vivid
devil	monstrous	superstition	weird

FA-5 Main Idea and Supporting Details

The **main idea** is the most important point of a story. **Supporting details** give more information about the main idea. These details usually answer questions like: *who, what, where, when,* and *why*. Read the following paragraphs. First make sure that the main idea is clear in your mind. Then look for supporting details that will give you information about the main idea.

> "I don't know what I'm going to do," Mrs. Rollins said quietly to the man sitting across the desk from her. Tears streamed down her cheeks as she tried to go on with her story.
>
> "Now, just keep talking. Tell me what's bothering you. It's my job to help," Mr. Harmon said kindly, his eyes full of understanding. After twenty years as a social worker, he could almost guess what Mrs. Rollins would say next.
>
> "My boy, Arvie. He's in bad company at the high school. The principal says he will fail unless his attendance improves and he starts doing some work in his classes. He says Arvie doesn't care about school. Arvie is interested only in fooling around and having a good time with his friends."

1. What is the main idea?
    a. Mr. Harmon is a kind and understanding man.
    b. Mrs. Rollins is very upset about her son and doesn't know what to do.
    c. The principal says Arvie will fail unless he improves.

2. What details support the main idea? Circle all the right answers.
    a. The man sat across the desk from her.
    b. Tears streamed down her cheeks.
    c. Mr. Harmon said, "Tell me what's bothering you."
    d. Mr. Harmon could guess what people would say next.

Assignment: Write a paragraph using as many of the words below as you can. State the main idea of your paragraph in the first or first two sentences and then include some supporting details in the sentences that follow.

accurate	cruise	naval	submarine
Aqua-Lung	depth	navigation	submerge
ascend	drench	observation	torpedo
capable	helm	species	transparent
confine	international	specimen	vibration

FA-6 Predicting Outcomes

When you are talking to a friend and that person stops in the middle of a sentence, you often know how your friend will finish the sentence. When you are reading a book, you might often figure out how the author will end that book. In both cases, you are **predicting**, or thinking ahead. When you predict, you use your knowledge and experience to think what might come next.

Read the following paragraphs. Then answer the questions and see if you can predict what will happen next.

Jack had been floating in the icy waters for hours. He held on tightly to the piece of wood that was holding him up. Even though his arms were aching, he considered himself lucky that he had been able to find something to grab hold of when the ship exploded and disappeared under the waves. He was getting more and more tired, and he hoped he would be able to keep from falling asleep. So far, he hadn't spotted any sharks.

He knew that the captain had been able to radio the ship's official position when it first ran into trouble. There was a good chance that help was already on the way and that it wouldn't be much longer before he would be rescued. Jack forced himself to stay awake.

Suddenly he thought he heard the sound of a propeller. He looked up and saw a helicopter. The words PATROL II were painted on it. He hoped the pilot would be able to see him in the water.

1. Jack felt that he had a chance of being rescued because
    a. Jack was a good swimmer.
    b. he hadn't spotted any sharks.
    c. the captain had radioed the ship's position before the ship went under.

2. What will happen next?
    a. The pilot will not see Jack and will keep on going.
    b. The helicopter will rescue Jack.
    c. The helicopter will crash into the ocean.

accomplishment	discourage	loosen	satisfaction
ascent	elevation	mountain	schedule
avalanche	grope	plateau	sheer
boost	jagged	portable	summit
clasp	location	remote	vertical

FA-7 Cause and Effect

A **cause** makes something happen. The result, or what happens, is the **effect**. In the sentence: "The ice and snow on the road caused the two cars to hit one another," the ice and snow on the ground is the cause and the two cars hitting one another is the effect. Words like *cause, as a result, lead to, thus, produce, therefore, so,* and *in order to* often tell us that an effect is coming. Words such as *because, since, due to,* and *as a result of* often tell us that a cause is coming.

Read the following paragraphs. Look for a cause and the effect of the cause.

> Have you ever heard of scurvy? Probably not, for it is a disease that people seldom get anymore. At one time, though, it caused severe sickness. It caused swelling, fever, bleeding gums, and teeth to fall out.
>
> At one time scurvy was common on ships that took long voyages. Because the sailors had no fresh fruits and vegetables for months at a time, many sailors perished from the disease.
>
> Today, we know that scurvy was caused by a lack of vitamin C. Scurvy can be prevented by eating fruits that contain high doses of vitamin C or by drinking the juice from these fruits.

1. Write <u>cause</u> or <u>effect</u> on the line.
   a. _____ The sailors had no fresh fruits and vegetables.
   b. _____ The sailors got a disease called scurvy.

2. What are the effects of scurvy? Check all the correct choices:
   a. _____ swelling and fever   d. _____ long ocean voyages
   b. _____ bleeding gums   e. _____ teeth fall out
   c. _____ blindness

Assignment: Use as many of these words as you can. Write a few paragraphs about some events and what caused them to happen. If you wish, you can use the words listed above to point to or signal each cause and each effect.

abundant	cultivate	gully	rural
alfalfa	domestic	livestock	rye
boundary	erosion	mechanical	slaughter
bulldozer	fowl	previous	trespass
conservation	grove	reap	variety

FA-8 Making Comparisons

We often **compare** two things to show how they are alike or how they are different. When we compare to show how things are alike, we use such words as *is similar to, like, in the same way,* or *both.* When we compare to show how things are different, we use such words as *on the other hand, is different from, yet, although, but, however, in fact,* and *instead.*

Read the following paragraphs. Then answer the questions to see how waterfronts of today were like those of many years ago and how they were different.

The waterfront swarms with people and machines. A dozen foreign languages fill the air with coarse sounds as sailors and workmen shout directions to each other through bullhorns. Telephone bells ring without stopping as foremen and shippers call in last-minute export orders.

Forklift trucks, piled high with packing cases, wheel their way between warehouse loading platforms and the docks. The drivers honk and hoot a path through a crowd of moving bodies, machines, and material.

Hundreds of years ago, the waterfront was also a busy place with workmen shouting directions to each other. But the sights and sounds were very different. Tall-masted wooden sailing ships creaked as they bumped against the wooden docks. Teams of men groaned under the weight of the heavy bales they carried. Sometimes, they even sang work songs to ease the backbreaking chore of loading the ships.

---

1. How are the waterfronts of today different from those of hundreds of years ago?
   a. They use machines to load the ships.
   b. Teams of men carry heavy bales on their back to load the wooden ships.
   c. They are not as busy as the waterfronts of a hundred years ago.

2. How are the waterfronts of today and long ago the same?
   a. They both need men to help give directions to load the ships.
   b. They both have wooden sailing ships tied up at the docks.
   c. Forklift trucks carry the packing cases from the warehouses to the docks.

Assignment: Using as many of the following words as you can, write a comparison between two things. Write one paragraph of ways in which the two things are alike and one paragraph of ways in which they are different.

actress	communication	mature	script
advertise	film	narrator	shutter
album	industry	photograph	studio
cartoon	interview	photographer	technical
commercial	lens	request	tense

FA-9 Summarizing

A **summary** tells in shorter form the important ideas and details of something you read or hear. When you write a summary, you must be careful to include only the important points and tell the events in the order in which they happened. Remember, the summary must contain only the main idea and the important details of the selection.

Read the following story. Then answer the question showing the best summary.

> The people who lived in the old mansion on Oak Street were very angry. Years before, the once well-kept building had been sold because the original owners could no longer afford to live there. The new owner divided the huge house into eight small apartments.
>
> Over time, the house began to wear out. The roof leaked, the paint peeled, and there was no hot water. Each month, the eight families paid their rent. Each month the owner promised to make the necessary repairs.

Which is the best summary?
1. When the old mansion on Oak Street was sold to the new owner, he divided it into small apartments.
2. The families who lived in the old house were angry because the owner never kept his promise to make repairs.
3. When a house is old it needs repairs.

Assignment: Read the following story. Then write a summary restating the main idea and including only the important details.

Once upon a time a pirate ship was wrecked on a small island far away from anywhere. Only a band of superstitious natives who believed in witches and devils lived on the island, so the pirate crew decided to take charge.

"That bunch is stupid," said a one-eyed pirate, "or else I'm the King of England."

"All natives are stupid," said the pirate captain. "We'll have to teach them how to work--for us! They'll be our slaves. This island will make a good kingdom for us."

So the captain put a crown of his best stolen jewels on his head and announced to the natives that he was their king.

Do this, do that! Get this, get that! The orders from the pirate king and his crew never stopped. So went the days and nights for several weeks, but the good life was not to last.

One night the king woke up from a nightmare. He had seen demons and phantoms dancing around his throne. They had long teeth like fangs and eyes that shot fire. They sang out with high, weird cries of warning: "Leave the island or you die!"

The king awoke trembling with fear. He sat up and was face to face with a skeleton. On its head sat the jeweled crown.

The demons and phantoms just like those in his dream came dancing into his room. "Leave the island!" they sang in their high, weird voices. The king jumped out of bed and ran for the door. Standing in the doorway was a demon with a gigantic, hideous head. It raised a menacing finger and pointed at the king. "Now you die," it cried.

The king waited no longer. Forgetting his crown of jewels, he leaped out of a window. Once outside, the king was joined by the entire pirate crew. All of them were racing wildly for the ocean. Leaping into the water, they swam and swam and swam. How far they got, no one knows.

After the pirates were out of sight, the natives came out laughing and talking to each other. "Well, now we can put away those demon costumes and skeletons until the next time."

FA-10 Making Inferences

When you read something, you make conclusions from what you read. Sometimes the information you need to make these conclusions is directly stated in what you read. Other times, the information is not directly stated. When the information is NOT directly stated, you must **make an inference.**

Read the following paragraphs. Then answer the inference question.

> The huge tanker was moving along steadily on course. It was headed for the Miami harbor. Suddenly, the captain looked out with horror. Directly ahead of the tanker was a fishing boat, an old, 55-foot fishing vessel.
>
> "My God!" yelled the captain. "What's the matter with them on that ship? Are they all asleep?"
>
> He knew what problems there were in getting his large tanker through these narrow waters, and the fishing craft was directly ahead. It would take his tanker half an hour and seven nautical, or navy, miles to come to a stop. If he tried to turn the tanker, it would have to swing around on a circle of many miles before it could change its course.

After the captain thought about his problem, what did he realize?
   a. There was a 55-foot fishing boat in the harbor.
   b. He could not turn or stop his ship in time to stop a crash.
   c. The tanker was headed for the Miami harbor.

Assignment: Using as many of the following words as you can, write a short story. Don't tell the reader everything that happened in the story. Then write a question or two asking the reader to make an inference about something that happened in the story.

amateur	dispute	manager	substitute
applause	extreme	referee	suspend
arena	fumble	regulation	tackle
athlete	idol	retire	trample
boardcast	injury	soccer	wealthy

FA-11 Setting

The **setting** of a story describes when and where the story takes place. A story can have one setting or it can have many settings. The writer can give you a lot of information about the setting or just enough so that you can infer what the setting is.

Read the following story. Then match the paragraph number with the setting described in that paragraph.

Paragraph 1

Have you ever heard of a volcano detective? That's what they call Haroun Tazieff. Whenever a volcano starts acting suspiciously or the earth starts shaking or lava (melted rock) starts pouring out of a volcano, chances are that Haroun Tazieff will be called to the region to study the situation.

Paragraph 2

Tazieff first became interested in volcanoes on March 1, 1948. He had been asked to study a volcano in the Congo that was erupting. That is, lava, steam, and ash from the volcano were bursting out of it.

Paragraph 3

The volcano that Tazieff is most familiar with is Mount Etna in Sicily. Because this volcano has been erupting since the Middle Ages, Tazieff has visited Etna about twice a year for the last thirty years. He calls it "my lab."

Paragraph 1   A volcano in the Congo
Paragraph 2   Mt. Etna is Sicily
Paragraph 3   Setting is not given

Assignment: Using as many of the following words as possible, write a short story that has at least three different settings.

ambulance	defense	headquarters	patriotic
armistice	destruction	honorable	rank
combat	doom	invade	resist
conquest	explosive	major	slain
courageous	fuse	minor	urgent

FA-12 Fact and Opinion

When someone says something that is true, we call this a **fact**. A fact can be checked with a source, by watching, or by experimenting. "There are seven days in a week" is an example of a fact.

An **opinion** is different from a fact. An opinion is something that is believed to be true. Very often you will find an opinion follows words such as *believe, think*, and *probably*. "I think Sunday is the best day of the week" is an example of an opinion. My opinion about which day is best might be different from yours.

Read the following paragraphs. Then label the statements as <u>fact</u> or <u>opinion</u>.

Young Elizabeth Blackwell was a very brilliant student, and she wanted more than anything to go to medical school to learn to become a doctor. It seemed impossible, for in the mid-1800s women were not allowed to go to most colleges, and certainly not to medical schools.

"It's not fair," said Elizabeth. "Women have the ability and the intelligence to be just as good doctors as men." But everywhere she went, the colleges told her that it would not be proper for women to become doctors. "It is proper that man be the doctor and woman the nurse," they said.

Years later, Elizabeth Blackwell became famous as the first woman doctor in America. Largely because of her achievements, women were able to go to college to become doctors.

Write fact or opinion.
1. _____ It is not proper for women to become doctors.
2. _____ It is proper that man be the doctor and woman the nurse.
3. _____ Women have the ability and intelligence to be just as good doctors as men.
4. _____ In the mid-1800s, women were not allowed to go to medical schools.
5. _____ Elizabeth Blackwell was the first woman doctor in America.

Assignment: Using as many of the following words as possible, write a short selection which includes at least three facts and three opinions.

acid	compound	false	normal
atom	disolve	fluid	percent
atomic	energy	funnel	quantity
bond	error	investigate	research
chemist	evaporate	mathematics	scientific

FA-13 Sensory Images

People have five **senses**: seeing, hearing, feeling, tasting, and smelling. When a writer uses words that make us think of any of these senses, the author is using **sensory images.**

Read the following paragraphs. Then write the correct sense for each sentence.

By the middle of the morning on April 6, 1909, Robert E. Peary, Matthew A. Henson, and four Eskimos had reached a position that they figured to be just three miles south of the North Pole. Although they were only a few miles from their goal, the men could not continue on. Ahead of them were frozen glaciers and icebergs. Howling gales and gusts of wind were echoing across the dreary region. The coldness was making them too stiff to keep walking.

The Eskimos made crude igloos, or snow houses, for everyone and then began a fire. The meat cooking in the igloo had a mighty good scent. After they had seen that the dogs were fed, the men were ready to eat a good meal. How delicious the food was!

---

see	hear	feel	taste	smell

1. _____ The coldness was making them too stiff to keep walking.
2. _____ Ahead of them were frozen glaciers and icebergs.
3. _____ Howling gales and gusts of wind were echoing across the dreary region.
4. _____ The meat cooking in the igloo had a mighty good scent.
5. _____ How delicious the food was!

Write fact or opinion.

1. _____ It is not proper for women to become doctors.
2. _____ It is proper that man be the doctor and woman the nurse.
3. _____ Women have the ability and intelligence to be just as good doctors as men.
4. _____ In the mid-1800s, women were not allowed to go to medical schools.
5. _____ Elizabeth Blackwell was the first woman doctor in America.

Assignment: Using as many of the following words as possible, write a short selection which includes at least three facts and three opinions.

acid	compound	false	normal
atom	disolve	fluid	percent
atomic	energy	funnel	quantity
bond	error	investigate	research
chemist	evaporate	mathematics	scientific

FA-13 Sensory Images

People have five **senses**: seeing, hearing, feeling, tasting, and smelling. When a writer uses words that make us think of any of these senses, the author is using **sensory images.**

Read the following paragraphs. Then write the correct sense for each sentence.

By the middle of the morning on April 6, 1909, Robert E. Peary, Matthew A. Henson, and four Eskimos had reached a position that they figured to be just three miles south of the North Pole. Although they were only a few miles from their goal, the men could not continue on. Ahead of them were frozen glaciers and icebergs. Howling gales and gusts of wind were echoing across the dreary region. The coldness was making them too stiff to keep walking.

The Eskimos made crude igloos, or snow houses, for everyone and then began a fire. The meat cooking in the igloo had a mighty good scent. After they had seen that the dogs were fed, the men were ready to eat a good meal. How delicious the food was!

see   hear   feel   taste   smell

1. _____ The coldness was making them too stiff to keep walking.
2. _____ Ahead of them were frozen glaciers and icebergs.
3. _____ Howling gales and gusts of wind were echoing across the dreary region.
4. _____ The meat cooking in the igloo had a mighty good scent.
5. _____ How delicious the food was!

Assignment: Using as many words from the following list as you can, write a short story that contains at least one sentence for each of the five senses.

ailing	diet	medical	reduce
artificial	fatal	operation	require
bleed	feeble	physician	swollen
constitution	invalid	posture	vein
crutch	joint	pulse	X-ray

Assignment: Using as many words from the following list as you can, write a short story that contains at least one sentence for each of the five senses.

ailing	diet	medical	reduce
artificial	fatal	operation	require
bleed	feeble	physician	swollen
constitution	invalid	posture	vein
crutch	joint	pulse	X-ray

FA-14 Author's Message

When an author writes something, he or she is trying to get a certain **message** across to the reader. This message might be a series of facts about something, it might be an explanation of something, or it might be a particular point of view.

Read the following story. As you read, see if you can find out what the author wishes to tell us about sports when Billie Jean was a young girl.

> The only thing that Billie Jean King ever wanted to be was a champion. Even back when she was an eleven-year-old child, she used to dream about being great in sports and being a great athlete. Her greatest desire was to be Number One!
>
> It wasn't easy for her, because when Billie Jean was going to school, to be interested in sports wasn't the thing for a girl to do. Sports were supposed to be for boys only. Girls were supposed to be charming and graceful, so people thought it was ridiculous for them to do anything physical. Everyone, even Billie Jean's mother, kept telling her, "Be more ladylike. Be a lady."

What does the author tell us about sports when Billie Jean was a young girl?
   a. Sports were only for girls.
   b. It was hard for a girl to be interested in sports because people did not think it was ladylike.
   c. Girls were supposed to be charming and graceful.

Assignment: Write a short essay about some topic of your choice. You can write about sports, television, or work. After you finish your essay, exchange papers with someone else who is working on this assignment. Then, each of you should write the "author's" message which you get when you read the essay written by the other person.

FA-15 Character and Feelings

A person's **character** is what makes that person act, feel, and think in a certain way. When you read a story, you can learn about a person's character by paying attention to what he or she says, thinks, and does. You can also learn about a character by what others say about that person.

A person's **feelings** are his or her emotions--anger, fear, happiness, and so on. When you understand how a character feels at certain points in a story, it is easier to understand why that person acts in a certain way. Sometimes the writer will tell you how a person feels, and sometimes you will have to figure it out from what that person says or does.

Read the following paragraphs about Juanita. Answer question 1 about paragraph 1 and question 2 about paragraph 2.

Paragraph 1

When Juanita was in kindergarten she decided to become a doctor. Her folks thought she would change her mind a dozen times before she got out of junior high school.

"There are lots of things to be when you grow up, Juanita," her mother used to say. "Just make sure you have a good education. I left college when I married your father and I wish I could go back."

Paragraph 2

By the time Juanita was in high school, her dream of being a doctor had become a real goal. She studied hard, working towards those high grades she knew she needed to enter college. Her room was full of books about how the human body worked. After school, she volunteered her time at the Children's Hospital.

1. Decide which statement describes Juanita best. (Paragraph 1)
   a. She is always changing her mind.
   b. She lets people make decisions for her.
   c. She makes up her own mind.

2. What have you learned about Juanita? (Paragraph 2)
   a. She is willing to work hard for what she wants.
   b. She doesn't care about other people.
   c. She spends her spare time doing things for herself.

Assignment: Use as many of the following words as possible and write two or three paragraphs describing the character and feelings of yourself, a friend, or a made up person.

allegiance	courteous	empire	privilege
ambition	disdain	fortress	shabby
baron	duchess	gallant	torture
beggar	duel	majestic	vow
betray	dungeon	oath	yield

FA-16 Understand Plot

The events in a story make up the **plot** of the story. A good plot is usually built around a conflict, or a struggle between two people, between two characteristics of the same person, or between a person and nature. For example, a conflict between two people could come from a situation between a worker and his or her boss. A conflict between two characteristics of the same person might come from a decision whether or not to stop smoking. Finally, an example of a conflict between a person and nature might come from someone trying to paddle a raft upstream on a very fast-moving river.

Read the following story. Try to find the conflict in the story that will help you identify the plot. Answer the question about the conflict.

Cal is a young man who has just completed a drug rehabilitation program. He now has a steady job and is saving money to continue his education. Although he doesn't know what he wants to do with his life, he does know that he wants to pass the highschool equivalency test. He also knows that he wants to stay off drugs.

One day while he was at work, an old buddy of his came to see him to try to get Cal involved in drugs again. It sounded tempting. They could go back to having the same kind of fun they used to have. Cal would be part of the gang again.

But Cal said no. He had gotten off drugs and had no desire to get hooked again. He called the security guard and had his "friend" removed. The more he thought about it, the more he realized that his friend really wasn't his friend after all.

The conflict in this story is an example of the conflict between
    a. two people.
    b. two characteristics of the same person.
    c. between a person and nature.

Assignment: Use as many of the words from the following list as possible and write a short story of three or four paragraphs in which you set-up a conflict either between two people, between two characteristics of the same person, or between a person and nature. Be sure to finish the story so we see how the conflict ends.

aircraft	destination	hangar	recommend
aviation	diagram	missile	regardless
aviator	formation	prevail	squadron
cockpit	frequent	promotion	warily
corps	goggle	radar	zig zag

FA-17 Methods of Persuasion

Very often the author of what you read or what you listen to is trying to **persuade** you to think in a certain way. When people run for political office, they hope to persuade voters to vote for them. Advertisers also try to get people to try their products by using various methods of persuasion. Some of the **methods of persuasion** that are used are:

Name Calling	Plain Folks
Glittering Generalities	Bandwagon
Transfer	Fear
Testimonial	

Read each of these sentences. On the numbered lines below the sentences, write the method of persuasion that is used in the sentence.

1. "My method of increasing taxes will bring steady economic growth without hurting the individual taxpayer."
2. "Everyone who lives in that neighborhood is rich, spoiled, and lazy."
3. "Buy High-Taste Orange Juice. It's the official juice of all astronauts."
4. "Martha Flick, star of stage, screen, and television, says that her favorite car is a Prestige Mobile."
5. "More drivers than ever before are using Slick motor oil."
6. "If you don't fasten your seatbelt the moment you get into your car, it may become too late."
7. "Senator Novote understands the problems of the cities. He lived in one for one year."

1. _____
2. _____
3. _____
4. _____

5. _____
6. _____
7. _____

Assignment: Using as many of the following words as possible, write a short essay trying to persuade someone to do or to buy something. Use as many of the methods of persuasion as you can.

assistant	conclusion	fake	liar
attendant	cunning	fascinate	mischievous
billion	deposit	gossip	resemble
bulletin	dignified	institute	skillful
conceal	disturbance	interfere	unravel

FA-18 Understanding Tone

The **tone** of a story is the mood of the story. For example, the tone can be happy, sad, funny, or exciting. The writer can tell us the tone of the story through words, such as cold and clammy, or through actions, such as the door slowly opened with a creak.

Read the following story. Then check the words that best tell the tone of the story.

> Sam Scott had always loved music and had always wanted to be a drummer. When he was a little boy growing up in South Boston, he and his friends Paul, Bob, and Karen would sit on his front steps and sing and clap out the rhythms of their favorite songs. They even made up some songs of their own.
>
> When the friends grew older, they saved their money and each bought an instrument. Paul bought an organ, Bob and Karen bought guitars, and finally Sam was able to afford the drums he had always wanted. They spent many hours rehearsing and soon got to be so good that people started asking them to entertain at parties and socials. Everyone liked their music. They called themselves The Group, and soon they were well known all over Boston. Everywhere they played, people would come from all over to hear them.

What is the tone? Check the two best answers.
   a._____ sad
   b._____ funny

   c._____ happy
   d._____ upbeat

   e._____ serious
   f._____ angry

Assignment: Using as many of the following words as possible, write a short essay that has a mysterious tone.

aft	marine	reckless	smuggle
ashore	moorings	reef	starboard
backward	outrigger	rogue	stow
gangplank	overboard	sensible	vicinity
harsh	prow	slavery	yacht

Usually when you read something, it contains many of the elements we have been learning about in these writing exercises. Read the following story. Then answer the questions. Note that each question examines a different skill.

One night last summer my throat felt like sandpaper and I had a heavy cough. I was smoking as usual. Something inside said it was time to stop smoking and so I made up my mind to try.

The next morning I faced my first test. Instead of having a smoke after breakfast, I took out a pack of hard candy. On the way to the bus stop, it seemed as though everybody I saw was smoking. I felt jumpy.

I was just as jumpy at work. I repair circuit boards for computers. You have to have a steady hand for that job. Well, the first morning my hands shook. I drank water and chewed gum to calm myself, but it didn't work. The rest of the day was no better.

The next morning things were no better. But after a few weeks, I no longer felt jumpy. Something else happened, too. My cough was gone, and my throat didn't feel rough. I was able to take longer walks without getting tired so quickly. And food tasted better than it had in years. Of course, I was also saving money.

Take it from an ex-smoker--a two-pack-a-day smoker--it pays to stop. And I'm not kidding.

1. How did the storyteller feel the first day she gave up smoking? (Tone)
   a. Happy   b. Nervous   c. Amused   d. Tired

2. Write the word cause or effect to show what each statement is.
   (Cause/Effect)
   a._____ The storyteller gave up smoking.
   b._____ The storyteller had a sandpaper throat and heavy cough.

3. What is the author's message?
   a. Smoking causes heart trouble and other illnesses.
   b. You have to have a steady hand to repair computer circuit boards.
   c. Giving up smoking isn't easy, but you can do it if you really try.

Assignment: Write an essay on a topic of your choice. Your essay should be at least four or five paragraphs. Include at least three of the following in your story:

facts
sequence
supporting details
context clues
predicting outcomes
cause and effect
comparisons

inferences
setting
character
sensory images
tone
persuasion
fact and opinion

FA-20 Drawing Conclusions

Sometimes when you read a story, whether it is true or made up, it is filled with facts and you can get a lot of information from what you read. When you think about this information, you can draw conclusions about the things you are reading about.

Reading the following two paragraphs. Then answer the question.

Everyone knows that alcoholism, or drinking too much, is a serious problem in this country. However, not all people who drink alcohol are alcoholics. There are millions of people in our country who drink moderately. That is, they drink only once in a while, they keep their drinking down to a safe amount, and they do not drive after they have been drinking.

The United States government has written a guide to instruct people on the effects of alcohol. This guide is called "U.S. Dietary Guidelines." It was written to demonstrate exactly what happens to the body when alcohol--in any amount--enters it.

From this story you can tell that

_____ a. it is perfectly all right to drink if you drink moderately.

_____ b. people who drink should get information on what happens to their bodies when they drink alcohol.

_____ c. the United States government believes that people shouldn't drink.

Assignment: Use as many of the following words as possible and write three or four paragraphs about a subject. Write in a way that lets a reader draw conclusions about the subject of your essay. After you finish your essay, write a question that will help the reader draw the conclusions.

absolutely	democratic	numerous	representative
association	essential	opposition	republic
citizenship	govern	parliament	sufficient
civilization	leadership	permanent	tyrant
democracy	majority	reform	union

FA-1
1. horizon
2. same
3. craters

FA-2
a. 2
b. 1
c. 3

FA-3
2

FA-4
1. that is
   the legends or stories
2. or
   stole by force
3. or
   battle

FA-5
1. b
2. b, c

FA-6
1. c
2. b

FA-7
1. a. cause
   b. effect
2. a, b, e

FA-8
1. a
2. a

FA-9
2

FA-10
b

FA-11
Paragraph 1... Setting is not given
Paragraph 2... Setting is not given
Paragraph 3... Mt. Etna is Sicily

FA-12
1. Opinion
2. Opinion
3. Fact
4. Fact
5. Fact

FA-13
1. Feel
2. See
3. Hear
4. Smell
5. Taste

FA-14
b

FA-15
1. c
2. a

FA-16
b

FA-17
1. Glittering generalities
2. Name calling
3. Transfer
4. Testimonial
5. Bandwagon
6. Fear
7. Plain Folks

FA-18
c, d

FA-19
1. b
2. a. Effect
   b. Cause
3. c

FA-20
b